EPOCHS IN THE LIFE OF JESUS

A STUDY OF DEVELOPMENT AND STRUGGLE IN THE MESSIAH'S WORK

A. T. ROBERTSON, M.A., D.D.,

BAKER BOOK HOUSE
Grand Rapids, Michigan

Paperback edition issued by
Baker Book House
with the permission of the
copyright owner, Cary Robertson

Second printing, July 1976

ISBN: 0-8010-7624-2

Printed in the United States of America

EPOCHS IN THE LIFE OF JESUS

TO

CHARLES E. TAYLOR

SOMETIME PRESIDENT OF

WAKE FOREST COLLEGE

PREFACE

I MAKE no apology for presenting another book on Jesus. The theme is exhaustless. Who can tell "the unsearchable riches of Christ"? Each age has to interpret Christ for itself. Indeed, each man has to do the same thing. We have passed through an age of acute criticism of the sources. The result, on the whole, has been exceedingly helpful. All that pertains to the historical aspects of Christ's career has been sifted. We know more of the times and the thought of the period. The background of the work of Christ is now well worked out. We are entering another period of theological controversy over the person of Christ. It is still the dominant issue in the thoughts of modern men.

This little book attempts a straightforward constructive discussion of the career of Jesus as set forth in the Gospels. There is no technical criticism of the sources, though the writer has reached his own conclusions on many points which come out incidentally. The eight chapters were delivered as popular lectures at a summer Chautauqua at Pertle

Springs, Mo., July, 1906, to an audience composed of ministers and a large and intelligent body of other Christian workers. The assembly requested the publication of the lectures. It is hoped that as published they may be useful to some who desire a positive presentation of the career of Jesus in the light of modern knowledge and in full sympathy with the position given to Christ in the Gospels.

No attempt is here made to tell the story of the life of Jesus, save as a brief summary now and then is necessary to the interpretation of that life. The attention is rather called to the movement and climacteric power in the career of Christ. The historic forces of that life seem narrow from one point of view, but the current runs deep and swift. The turning points in the life of Christ are brought out sharply with less accent on other things, so that one may the better feel the titanic struggle that Jesus had with ecclesiastical tyranny and bigotry. If the reader can thus "realize" Jesus, he will find the Gospels luminous with fresh light. The lumber of learning is all left out here, that the attention of the reader may be focussed on Christ, who battled for human freedom in the most heroic of all conflicts. He won the freedom of the human spirit at the greatest possible cost. The Gentiles can now indeed see Jesus without throwing any preachers into a panic.

The whole world can now see Christ, if forsooth
men have eyes to see. "In the midst of you standeth one whom ye know not" (John 1 : 62).

I might add that for twenty years I have been
teaching theological students "the things of Christ."
I give no bibliography, but my obligations to the
great writers on the Life of Christ are too numerous
to mention. I cannot, however, forbear acknowledg-
ing my debt to the matchless teaching of John A.
Broadus in this institution. But the Gospels themselves have been my chief inspiration in this study.

A. T. ROBERTSON.

LOUISVILLE, KY.,
SEPTEMBER, 1907.

TABLE OF CONTENTS

EPOCHS IN THE LIFE
OF JESUS

CHAPTER I

THE MESSIANIC CONSCIOUSNESS OF JESUS

"This is my beloved Son, in whom I am well
pleased" (Matt. 3:17).

THERE are many ways of approaching the life of
Jesus. No other theme has produced so many
books, and the steady stream flows on. The
knowledge of Jesus is indeed the most excellent of
the sciences. And yet no one has written an ex-
haustive or comprehensive discussion of Christ. It
has always been so. No one of the Gospels gives
a complete picture of the Master, nor do all four
Gospels tell us all that we should like to know, nor,
in fact, all that was once known of Jesus. Herein
lies a strong argument for the deity of Christ, his
inexhaustibleness. "The riches of Christ" are
"unsearchable" and past finding out.

1. *The Problem of Jesus.*—He is a constant chal-

lenge to men, to the greatest of men. It was so at
the first and is true to-day. Men have grappled
with the universe under the spell of a great theory
of development. Orderly development has been
found in the various spheres of human knowledge.
But what about Jesus of Nazareth? Is he the prod-
uct of the narrow ceremonialism and ecclesiastical
bigotry of Palestinian Pharisaism? No connection
can be traced between Christ and Plato, Socrates,
Buddha, or any of the great thinkers outside of
Judaism. Here is universal and absolute truth that
sprang out of an atmosphere of intense racial pride
and hate. Here is the man who laid most stress
on the spiritual and moral aspects of religion in the
midst of teachers who tithed mint, anise and cumin.

But this is not all. Here is one who led a sinless
life in the face of malignant enemies, whose character
is the unapproachable ideal of all men who have ever
read his story. Here is one who made the greatest
claims for himself, who put himself on a par with the
living God, according to the testimony of the Gospels
which bring us the story of his career. Here is one
who asserts his right to the allegiance of all men,
who offers to rescue all that come to him from sin
and its effects. His perfect life and his lofty teachings give a serious aspect to what would otherwise
be absurd claims.

The tremendous power of Jesus over the world commands respect, whatever the explanation. The men who are most loyal to Christ are just the men who have been foremost in the advancement of civilization and the uplift of the race. The nations where the influence of Jesus is greatest are those whose people stand highest among the kingdoms of earth. The Protestant nations which have freedom from priestly domination have long led the world.

Even those who reject the claims of Jesus to deity on philosophical grounds, like Prof. G. B. Foster (following Pfleiderer), or on critical grounds by disposing of the evidence for his career, like Prof. N. Schmidt (following Bousset and Wrede), are reverent in their treatment of the person of Jesus, even enthusiastic about his character.

"What think ye of Christ?" He was indeed set for the falling and the rising of many not only in Israel, but in all the world. He is the loadstone of human hearts, the test of every man's life. Like Charles Lamb, we all feel that if Jesus came into our presence we should instinctively kneel. Jesus presses himself upon our hearts and upon our minds. He does not expect us to give up our reason when we come to settle the question with him. We need then all the intellect that we have. The difficulty is to see the problem as a whole and as it really is.

In this study we seize the main things in their historical development and seek to grasp their relation to
each other and their results.   No merely natural explanation of Jesus is possible.   It is irrational, in
view of all the facts, to attempt it.   A "greater than
Jonah" is here, the Son of God.   Men have not always been able to show Jesus to those who asked to
see him.   Philip and Andrew were puzzled over the
simple and polite request of the Greeks.   Sometimes
our sermons hide Christ, alas, instead of revealing
him.   Our theology may become a veil that rests on
the heart so that Jesus is not seen when the Gospel
is read.   Our wranglings may picture an absent
Christ and reflect the ecclesiastical ambitions of the
first disciples instead of the spiritual elevation of
Jesus.

The search-light of modern historical investigation
has brought out into clearer relief the historic Christ
and his environment.   We can go back behind
Calvin and Augustine to Christ.   We can even go
behind Paul, Peter and John to Christ himself.   We
can see how each of the Apostles apprehended Jesus,
what each contributed to our knowledge of the
Master.   We can see how they at first were daz-
zled by the great Light that bewildered them,
how gradually they came to understand him and
his message and their mission.   The revolution

wrought in the first disciples is the eternal miracle of Christianity and is repeated every day of the world.

It is the vision of the Eternal Christ. We cannot put mere historical limitations around Jesus in our study of him. While we follow the struggle, the greatest of the ages, which he made with the human and superhuman forces about him, we are conscious of a higher element in him. He himself spoke of this transcendent fact, and it puzzled and dazed all around him. His life did not begin when he was born, nor did it end when he died. To-day the world bows not before a hero of hate whose body still lies on Golgotha's hill, but before the Risen Christ who sits on the throne of majestic glory at the right hand of the Father. That is the New Testament picture of the Redeemer who has triumphed over death and the grave and who is leading a victorious warfare against the hosts of evil. This is the Saviour from sin who has spoken peace to our hearts and in whose name we work to-day. So, while we study together the human conditions and the various historic epochs in the career of Christ, let us not think that such an attempt can explain all that is true of Jesus then and now. But let our hearts burn within us as Jesus comes and walks with us and talks with us as we seek to explain some of the mystery of the Nazarene.

2. *The First Glimpse of Jesus.*—When the boy Jesus comes to Jerusalem at twelve years of age, he knows that he is the Son of God in a sense not true of other men. "Wist ye not that I must be in my Father's house?" His parents were astonished at the ease and powers he showed in such a place of dignity, teaching and amazing the doctors of divinity in the rabbinical theological seminary. But none the less is he astonished at their ignorance of the fact that this is the place of all the world for him. Who can tell a boy's golden dreams of the future till some day the sun bursts out in full glory? The boy has gone forever with the revelation of the man, and the manly purpose has come to fill the heart and life. The word "must" throws a long light back into the boy's quiet years at Nazareth. Modern theologians speculate learnedly on the time when Jesus first became conscious of the fact that he was God's Son and had a Messianic mission to perform. That is idle speculation. We only know that at twelve years of age Jesus is aware that God has laid his hand upon him. He is at home in the Father's house and rejoices to discuss high and holy themes.

The whole problem of the person of Jesus is brought before us by this incident. By the side of this early Messianic consciousness lies the other fact that he grew in wisdom and in stature. He was a real boy for all the divine element in him, and an obedient one, too, for he was subject to his parents gladly after this event. The one boy that really knew more than his father and mother was a model of obedience.

The loneliness of the boy Jesus at this time impresses one. He was not understood by the theological professors at Jerusalem, nor by his parents, not even by his mother who had long ago been told of the future of her child. Had she hid her secret so deep in her heart that it was well-nigh lost? But the time was long and he probably did little, if aught, out of the ordinary, certainly none of the silly things told by the apocryphal gospels. Only once is the veil lifted during the silent thirty years, and thus light shines on the Messianic consciousness of Jesus. He had a human education those years at Nazareth, in his home, in the synagogue, in the fields with the birds and flowers, with his playmates, at his work in the carpenter's shop.

Luke is the writer of this incident, and it is he whose introduction is so much like that of the Greek historian Thucydides. Luke it is who said that he had made careful examination of the sources and had taken pains to be accurate. The stamp of truthfulness is on the narrative with its simplicity and reality. Mary herself may well have told Luke what is here narrated. It is the fashion to-day with some to discount what John has to say about Jesus, but this is Luke the historian.

A word is needed in passing concerning the naturalness and reality of a life that is so soon conscious of a high mission. The explanation lies in the appeal to the facts. There is no vestige of artificiality, of playing a part, in the career of Jesus. We drop out of sight as wilfully blind those who deny that Jesus ever thought that he was the Messiah, who even say that the Old Testament does not predict a Messiah. This surprising result is obtained either by rejecting the passages or by marvellous exegesis of everything that points to a Messiah. It is not strange that God's Son should be acquainted with his Father. What better place for that consciousness to come to larger and more vivid activity than in the temple of the people of God, dedicated to the worship of God?

This boy of twelve who loved the birds and the flowers and worked well at the carpenter's trade grew in favor with God and with men. And no wonder. He combined early piety with popularity. When Joseph died he doubtless became in a sense the mainstay of his mother. Did ever mother's heart have so much to make her glad? or so much that she did not understand in her wonderful boy?

3. *Was Jesus Born of a Virgin?*—We purposely

passed over his birth till now. This has become an acute question in our time. The scientific temper demands to know everything and sometimes thinks it has succeeded; but this feeling of omniscience is not monopolized by the scientific spirit. The X-rays, wireless telegraphy, radium, and radiobes, to go no further, make it difficult to-day for the real scientist to say what can and what cannot happen in nature, even if God does not exist. If God does exist, there is no real difficulty from God's point of view.

Now Matthew and Luke both give the story of the supernatural birth of Jesus, but from different points of view; Luke from the standpoint of Mary, Matthew from that of Joseph. Evidently there are therefore two independent accounts of this great event, both of which come from sources near Jerusalem, while James and Jude, brothers of Jesus, still lived, and possibly while Mary, the Mother, survived. Luke spent two years in Cæsarea, and was a careful historian. In the opening chapters of his Gospel which tell of this wondrous event there are signs that he used an Aramaic or Hebrew document or heard the story from one who spoke Aramaic. The very first thing told, after his careful historical introduction, is the birth narrative. There are miracles here recorded, not necessarily beautiful legends

to idealize or deify Jesus.   Legends would be possible
if the incarnation of Jesus were inherently impossible.   But who can say that with confidence?

The silence of Mark cannot be turned against
Matthew and Luke. This Gospel was probably
written in Rome under the influence of Peter and
away from the Jerusalem circle.   It is not surprising that nothing should be said at first in public concerning the true birth of Jesus. He passed as the
son of Joseph and Mary. The new Syriac manu-
script of Matthew from Sinai does say that Joseph
begat Jesus in one passage, but in another place the
old reading is left. The text was probably under
Ebionitic influence which denied the deity of Jesus.

If the prologue of John, with its wondrous survey
of the pre-incarnate state of Jesus, does omit a discussion of the birth of Jesus and so has nothing concerning the Virgin Birth, it is not to give us an easier
interpretation of the origin and person of Christ.
Certainly John, for I do not doubt that he wrote the
Fourth Gospel, does not circumscribe the career
nor the person of Jesus within purely human limits.
The earthly career of Jesus is but a very small though
momentous portion of the eternal existence of the Son
of God, who was with the Father in heaven before
the incarnation and who has returned to the Father
since the resurrection and ascension.   It is not mere

ideal pre-existence that John has here in mind, but
personal presence with the Father. John goes further still. He says pointedly of the Logos: *He was
God*. That is a conception capable of comprehen-
sion, that the Father should have a Son, a necessary
corollary of Father in fact. But John even says
that this Son or Logos became flesh and dwelt
among us. The Son of God, who was God and co-
existed with the Father, became flesh. How? I
venture to ask. Was it a mere theophany? Was
Jesus a real man? Were the Docetic Gnostics right
after all who held that Jesus only seemed to be a
man? The proper interpretation of John's language
is found in the Virgin Birth, and only thus. He
assumes it as well known and implies it. If he were
in truth the son of Joseph, he would not be "God
only begotten" (true text).

The difficulty is just as great if we turn to Paul.
He does say that Jesus was born of woman, and
thus disposes of Docetic Gnosticism. He was a
real man according to Paul. But did Paul hold him
to be God as John clearly believed? He does not
use the term God of Jesus unless we so punctuate
Rom. 9 : 5, and read church of God (correct text)
in Acts 20 : 28. But in Col. 1 : 15-18 and elsewhere
(as in II. Cor. 8 : 9 and Phil. 2 : 6.) Paul so de-
scribes Jesus that he can be to him nothing else but

God. Paul may or may not have faced the question
of the Virgin Birth of Jesus. But the real deity of
Jesus is taught by Paul, and that is the *crux* of the
whole matter. He has nothing inconsistent there-
with, nor has John. All the positive testimony of
the New Testament is in favor of this explanation,
and there is not a word against it. Indeed, the
theological conceptions of Paul and John demand
it. Professor Briggs (in *North American Review*
for June, 1906) boldly claims that to give up the
Virgin Birth is to give up the philosophical basis for
the incarnation of Christ. One may still believe in
the deity of Jesus and be illogical. That does not
disturb a good many people. Logic cuts a small
figure in a good deal of theology. But it is not possible to think of God becoming man except by the
Virgin Birth and not thereby have two persons in
the one into whom God has entered. The heresy
of Nestorianism or two persons in Christ is then
inevitable. And even if God could thus enter such
a man, he would not thereby affect any other man.
If Jesus is indeed the God-Man, Son of God and
Son of Man, the Virgin Birth is the only conceivable
way for that great event to happen. And, indeed,
this problem is no more difficult than anything else
connected with the deity of Jesus. *That* is the
problem after all. The ancient deification of the

Roman emperor and other heroes and demi-gods does not prove that this is what happened with Jesus.

So let us take our place with the shepherds on the hills of Bethlehem and hear the angels sing about peace on earth to men who receive the good pleasure of God. Let us fall under the spell of this transcendent mystery. The Child in the Manger has brought new hope to every mother in the world, new glory to every child on earth, new dignity for every man who has felt the touch of the Son of God. He will indeed save his people from their sins. Zacharias and Mary, Simeon and Anna caught a glimpse of the Light that brightens Jew and Gentile. They sang the first Christian hymns. They had seen the salvation of Israel. The wise men still fall at his feet, and the Herods and Satan are still trying to compass the ruin of the Christ. But not priest, nor king, nor devil can stay the march of the Kingdom of God.

Who is Jesus then? No doctrine that we can frame meets all the facts. The Kenosis theories of the humiliation of Christ put into Paul's word in Phil. 2 : 9 more than he had. They multiply, not minimize, the problems. They fade away into dimness and vagueness. Of what did Christ empty himself when he left the place beside the Father on high?

Did it apply to his divine nature or only to his divine glory? How much of God's knowledge and God's power did Christ have while he was man? How could the infinite Son of God tie himself up in human flesh with human limitations? How could the sinless one dwell in flesh and not have sin? If he had sin, he could not save us from sin. If the true theologian is humble and reverent here, it must be recalled that the true scientist is not boastful about life, ultimate life, the Source of all things. We do not understand either half of this problem, God or man. It is not strange that the combination causes new difficulties. Perhaps when we do reach clearness of vision about both God and man, we shall approach the subject of the God-Man with more confidence. At any rate, we are sure that this sublime union of God and man does offer the only real solution of the career and character of Jesus of Nazareth. It is in personality that God and man can properly meet. Philosophy can help a little way here by the new emphasis on the problems of personality. We can in Christ form an intelligible conception of God. Without Christ our ideas of God tend to fade away into abstractions.

4. *The Father's Sanction of the Son.*—The news came to Jesus in Nazareth that strange things were going on down by Jordan river. He was a man

now, the man Jesus, and the news had a fascination
for him. It was not the call of the wilderness, but
the call of his Father that he heard, though he must
go to the desert. A new prophet had appeared in
the wilderness, a man with odd garments, queer
habits, and a marvellous message. But the charm
of John was not in his garb nor in his diet. Greatness cannot be counterfeited by imitating eccen-
tricities. It was the spirit and power of Elijah, not
the hairy raiment of Elijah, that most characterized
the Baptist. The message was the most wonderful
thing about the man. He said that the Kingdom
was at hand, no longer in the distant future. Was
it true? The news spread till all Jerusalem and
Judea went out to see what was more than a reed
shaken in the wind. Finally the preachers and
teachers went also with the crowd to hear this mountain prophet, some perhaps to scoff and sneer. It
was amazing, the audacity of the man! He said
that even the preachers must repent like common
sinners, publicans and Gentiles, and be baptized.
As if we were not the children of Abraham! But
this prophet spared not high nor low, soldier, publican, nor priest. Those that repented he immersed
in the Jordan, and the new rite made many suppose
that he was the Messiah himself. For a little while
then John was taken at more than his real value

(as reformers often are), but he soon dispelled such false estimates by bluntly saying that he was not the Messiah. He was only the Voice of the Herald crying in the wilderness. He was not worthy to unloose the shoes of the Messiah, who would have the baptism of the Holy Spirit. But where was the Messiah?

Did Jesus tell his mother where he was going when he left Nazareth? His crisis had come and he knew it. John and Jesus met by the water side. John had had a sign given him by which to recognize the Messiah. Doubtless he had each day watched for that sign as he baptized the multitudes and eagerly scanned each upturned face. He probably had not seen Jesus, certainly not for a long time, and he did not know who the Messiah was. But before the sign came he had an instinctive feeling that here was he! It was incongruous that the Messiah should ask baptism at his hands. John had not, it seems, been himself baptized. His baptism called for confession of sin, and in the presence of the sinless One, John felt afresh his own unworthiness and asked baptism at the hands of Jesus. But Jesus held his ground. It was right enough for John to feel that way, but Jesus was a man and a Jew and must obey the call that his Father made on all to be baptized on confession of sin. The fact that he had no sin to

confess did not relieve him from the obligation to do
this righteous act of obedience. Let us never forget that Jesus thought it worth while to come from
Nazareth to the Jordan, not to be saved, for he needed
no saving, and baptism saves no one except symbol-
ically. He gave the sanction of his own example to
baptism in the Jordan, and later he enjoined it
upon all his disciples. He was indeed in a symbolic
way setting forth his own death and resurrection
also, but John in all likelihood did not see that
point.

John soon saw that Jesus was right in being baptized, for the Father spoke audibly to the Son, and
the Spirit of God in the form of a dove rested on
Jesus as he came out of the water praying. It was
an august moment. Father, Son, and Spirit join
in celebrating this event. Clearly the baptism of
Jesus had a wonderful personal significance. It has
been variously interpreted. Some imagine that now
for the first time Jesus became aware of the fact
that he was the Messiah, the Son of God, but that
interpretation is not justified by the facts. His protest to John just before the baptism was no disclaimer
of the Messiahship. His whole bearing with John
was that of one who had faced his destiny and had
settled it. Some of the Cerinthian Gnostics imagined that the Christ as an Aeon or Emanation of

God came down on Jesus at his baptism like a dove, and that it was this Aeon Christ that was divine, while Jesus was himself a mere man. His baptism was, however, the beginning of the public Messianic work. Jesus was now stepping out into the open. He had crossed the Rubicon and there was no turning back. He had put his hand to this plow and he must follow it to the end and sink the plow in deep. It was the coming of the Holy Spirit that constituted the anointing of Jesus, and not the baptism. Let us not confuse the two things. We may compare the prophetic endowment in the Old Testament.

5. *The Moral Issue in the Temptation.*—The Gospel writers can only have gotten this narrative from Jesus himself. He probably told the disciples long afterwards about this fierce struggle with the prince of evil that met him at the threshold of his ministry, as it often comes just then to the young preacher. Mark barely mentions the fact, while Matthew and Luke tell the details of the Titanic struggle. The time of the occurrence could only be at the beginning of the ministry. Satan would wish at once to challenge the Messiah. Like a lion of the jungle he challenges the newcomer into his domain. Rightly or wrongly the devil claimed this world as his own. He had done much to make it a jungle of sin and woe. He felt that there could only be enmity

between himself and Jesus. The Synoptic Gospels all agree in putting the temptation just after the baptism. It was the psychological moment. Every new convert has a fresh struggle with the devil after his baptism. "Now, you have gone and made a fool of yourself," the devil will say.

We may not pause to discuss whether it was an objective visitation of the devil or merely the pressure of devilish suggestion on the mind of Jesus. Most probably both elements existed. It is no more difficult to think of the devil making a visible manifestation of himself to Jesus than to believe in the existence of the devil at all. That is the real problem. If there is a real spirit of evil who has access to and power over the soul of man, we need trouble ourselves little about the rest. It would be comforting to believe, as some writers do, that the devil is dead. Certainly sin is not dead. If there is no devil, it is not complimentary to man to make him originally responsible for all the evil in the world. But, whether the devil appeared objectively to Christ or not, it was in the realm of spirit that the temptation took place. Mark even says that Jesus was led of the Spirit into the wilderness to be tempted of the devil. This is at first a hard saying, but probably it only means that God wished his Son to meet the tempter at once and have it out once for all. Not that the devil would not try again, but the line for future conflict would be clearly defined.

The devil has an evident allusion to the approval of the Father at Christ's baptism when he said "if thou art a son of God," as God had said. Not that the devil denies that this is so; in fact, the form of the condition implies that it is true, and he says "a son of God," not "the Son of God," as God had said. But he suggests to Jesus that it would be just as well for him to test what God had said. That would do no harm. He would then have personal experience to sustain him. He was very hungry and, if he was God's Son, surely he could do creative work as God did. It was a subtle appeal. Jesus would work miracles for others. Why not begin by working one for himself? In a word, shall Jesus be a selfish Messiah? But the temptation would have been no temptation put in that form. That is the peril with a temptation, that its real character is at first concealed and difficult to see. There was here concealed distrust of God.

The Jews expected the Messiah to come with a great spectacular display. They will often ask Jesus to do a sign, not merely work miracles, but some great portent in the heavens, for instance. The devil suggests that Jesus accommodate himself to the popular expectation and let them see him come sailing down from the pinnacle of the temple, right out of heaven. They would hail him with acclaim. But Jesus was to be no mere performer of tricks, no balloon or parachute aeronaut. The devil grows pious and quotes Scripture, not misquotes it as some good people do, but he misapplies it. In that also the devil has no monopoly. But Jesus saw that he would be presumptuous and not trustful if he dared such a feat. Besides, he might as well settle now as later whether he was to be the kind of a Messiah that the people wished or the one that the Father had planned. Every preacher in a humbler way has to meet a similar problem. It is so easy to fall in with the drift of things, so easy as to fall over a great height when nervous and afraid.

But the devil was not done. He appealed to the ambition of Jesus. He would help him to be king of the world. The devil was an old hand at it. He would not exactly abdicate; he and Jesus could run it together. That would be better than open war. He offered Jesus all the kingdoms of the world and the glory of them. It was a fascinating picture as it passed before the mind of Jesus. He only asked in return that Jesus bow down before him up here on the mountain. Nobody else was there, and it would merely be a recognition of the facts of the case. The devil *did* have the kingdoms of the world in his

power, the great Roman Empire, for instance.
Was it not better to make peace and be friends than
to fight it out? He could turn this great Roman
Empire against Jesus, who had no disciples as yet,
and, if he should win some, he could use this empire against the Kingdom of Jesus. This was the
heart of the temptation. Jesus wanted the world.
In fact, he had come to win the world, but he was
to win the world from the devil, not take the world
on the devil's terms and with the devil as dictator.
Christ was not confused by the issue. He knew
what his decision meant. But he loved the world
too well to betray it in that fashion. He would not
have a mixture of the kingdom of heaven and the
kingdom of the world. He would die for the world.
Strange to say, the devil did fight Jesus with the
Roman Empire and did graft much of the world on
the church of the Middle Ages. But Jesus brushed
aside all compromise and surrender and ordered
Satan to go hence. He did go, cowed for the moment, but he will bide his time and wait for another
chance. Death then faces Jesus at the very beginning. He must be willing to die for men before he
can save men. So Jesus chose the high and stony
path that led to Calvary, a lonely way and a weary
one. His decision meant eternal conflict with Satan
till he has conquered and the kingdoms of this world

have become the kingdom of our Lord and of his Christ.

6. *The Johannine Presentation of Jesus.*—It harmonizes with the synoptic picture as seen in the temptation, for instance. In John, Jesus is represented as conscious from the very start that he is the Messiah charged with a mighty work for God, conscious also of his death for men. The point to note is that this conception of Christ is given also in the Synoptic Gospels. John has merely accented what is implicit in the temptation and expressed by the Father at the baptism. Jesus is the Son of God. John represents Christ as addressed as Messiah and even claiming to be Messiah at the first. That is not strange, but natural. Just as John tells of the early baptizing done by the disciples of Jesus, which apparently ceased because of the popularity of Jesus with the people and consequent hostility of the Pharisees, so he narrates the early Messianic claims which were soon stopped in terms and for the same reason. The collision with the rulers at Jerusalem at the very first passover made it plain that matters would come to a focus at once if Jesus persisted in openly claiming to be the Messiah or in allowing himself to be so called. The Messianic restraint of Jesus, therefore, became a necessity. But this restraint does not at all mean that Jesus began

his public career merely as another rabbi or even a
prophet like John looking for the Messiah, finally
drawn by popular expectation to think he was the
Messiah or to pose as the Messiah. Those alterna-
tives are alike inconceivable and inconsistent with
all that we know of Jesus. He was no mere dreamer,
no fanatic, no play-actor, no demagogue, no char-
latan. There are difficulties in thinking of Jesus
as knowing at the beginning of his ministry that he
was the Messiah and would be put to death, but that
fate is before every true soldier. Jesus goes on
bravely to meet his hour and live out his day. Actual experience shows that the highest type of man-
hood is developed in a time of stress and storm.

7. *The Terms Used of Jesus Have a Peculiar Interest.*—His own favorite word, Son of Man, had a
Messianic import, though not generally so understood at the time. It served as a claim for his office,
and yet in a veiled form. It was certainly more than
the jejune Aramaic "barnasha," a man. In some
passages that idea is positively ridiculous. Besides, the term accents the incarnation of Christ.
He is the representative man. A few times Jesus
called himself the Son of God (Synoptic as well as
Johannine) in a sense not true of other men. This
claim the Jews regarded as blasphemy, for he
claimed to be equal with God and received worship

as God. After the opening ministry he did not allow himself to be called Messiah in so many words till he pointedly asked Peter to say what he thought of him. Even then he warned Peter and the disciples not to call him Messiah in public. And yet on oath before the Sanhedrin, Jesus did say that he was the Messiah, the Son of God, and the Son of Man. He paid the penalty of that confession by death. It would not be blasphemy for the real Messiah to make this claim. And Jesus had been identified by John the Baptist as the Lamb of God that taketh away the sin of the world. The last time that the Baptist saw the Messiah he stood looking, rapt with the glory of the vision. "He standeth in the midst of you," he had said, "and ye know him not." And that is often true to-day of the unseen and unrecognized Christ.

CHAPTER II

THE FIRST APPEAL OF JESUS

"Come, and ye shall see" (John 1:39).

We are told in Heb. 5:8 that, though Jesus was a son, yet he learned obedience by what he suffered. He had to be made perfect by the discipline of experience (Heb. 2:10). Thus alone he could become the Captain (or Author) of salvation, and thus he could gain power to help the tempted (Heb. 2:18). Experience does not come as a gift or an inheritance, nor can it be bought. Already Jesus has settled accounts with the great tempter as to the character of his work. The long war for the rescue of the world has begun, for Jesus came to bring not peace, but a sword.

1. *Connection with John the Baptist's Work.—* Christ was not wholly alone in his work for the Kingdom of God. A few spirits like Simeon and Anna, Zacharias and Elizabeth, of a former generation, lingered on, waiting for the consolation of Israel, though as a whole the "seed-plot of Christianity" in Sanday's words was in uncongenial soil.

26

But John the Baptist, as the Forerunner of the
Messiah, had brought to the surface some choice
spirits who would hail the Messiah with joy.

John the Baptist never wavered for a moment
about the Messiah. He could take his own measure
perfectly, a very difficult thing to do. We make
mental misfits very easily. He did not allow flattery
or intrigue to turn him from hearty loyalty to Jesus
as the true Messiah, the Hope of Israel. The Gospel of John does not narrate the baptism of Jesus
by the Baptist, though it implies it in alluding to the
sign of the Holy Spirit descending on him (1: 33).
After the baptism of Jesus, John only saw him
twice, so far as we know, and that on two successive
days. But on each occasion his soul was rapt with
the vision. There is the Lamb of God! Naught
else was worth seeing while Jesus was to be seen.
"He looked upon Jesus as he walked" (John 1: 36).
He rejoiced to bear his testimony of identification.
"I have seen, and I have borne witness that this is
the Son of God" (John 1: 34). He saw truly also
the sacrificial aspect of the Messiah's work. He is
"the Lamb of God that taketh away the sin of the
world" (John 1: 29). The Baptist did not, as
some maintain, wholly mistake the work of the Messiah, for he expressly said that Jesus would perform
a spiritual ministry (baptize with the Spirit), though

his coming did bring inevitable judgment upon the world.

2. *The First Disciples.*—These were disciples of the Baptist, Andrew and probably John the Evangelist, who took the Baptist at his word and went with Jesus. It was a moment of great significance for Jesus. Here at least was a beginning, two souls prepared by the Baptist's work. John the Evangelist wrote of it when an old man, but he never forgot across the years the event nor the hour of the day, ten o'clock in the morning (Roman time). They spent the day with Jesus, the first of many like days. The leaven of the Kingdom was already at work. To Andrew belongs the distinction of moving first to win another. The correct text (John 1: 41) indeed says that this is the first thing that Andrew did after his communion with Jesus. He put first things first. He had no time for aught else. To Simon, his brother, he says simply: "We have found the Messiah." It was a piece of tremendous news. Could it be true? Simon is soon face to face with Jesus. At once the eye of Jesus was taken with the man. He "looked upon him" with all the penetration of human nature so characteristic of Christ. He saw in Simon what nobody else had ever seen—saw indeed the instability, the impulsiveness, the weakness of his nat-

ure, but saw beyond all that the deeper and
stronger possibilities of this man and appealed, as
he always does, to the best in him. He prophesied
a new name for Simon, that of Cephas or Peter.
He did not now deserve to be called a Rock, but he
will. What Jesus did with Simon he does with every
man. The most remarkable thing about Jesus is
what he puts into a man, not what he sees in him.
Thus Christ has lifted up the world, by finding the
best thing in a man, developing that, and putting
new life into him, the Kingdom of God.

On the next day Jesus finds Philip and pointedly
says: "Follow me." It was a strange command.
Philip did not know Jesus. Why should he follow
this stranger? He may have been a disciple of the
Baptist, but at any rate Philip came from Bethsaida, the town of Andrew and Peter, who were now
with Jesus. This fact gave weight to the demand
of Jesus. So it is to-day. We follow Christ partly
because our friends do. Besides, there was a tone
of insistence in the words of Jesus. He seemed to
have the right to ask this supreme service of Philip.
Men will listen to the plea of Jesus, it is now clear.
It will be possible to win men to the Kingdom of
Christ in opposition to the kingdom of the devil.

As Andrew (and probably also John the Evangelist) was stirred by the power of the leaven, so Philip

is stirred to find Nathanael. *Each one wins one.*
Why not? That is the normal work of the Kingdom of God. "We have found him," Philip says.
Εὑρήκαμεν. It was the greatest of earth's discov-
eries. Not gold, nor diamond, nor planet, nor new
sun, nor radium can be mentioned beside this discovery of whom Moses and the prophets did write.
But Nathanael was not impulsive like Simon. He
was a sceptic. "Can any good thing come out of
Nazareth?" (John 1 : 43). Like many other sceptics, he settled the whole matter on a side issue.
Philip had called him "Jesus of Nazareth, the Son
of Joseph." Nathanael lived not far from Nazareth. To be a citizen of that town was enough for
him. Nazareth had a bad name, and was the
wrong place anyhow according to the Old Testament; therefore the Messiah could not live there.
Logic is after all a poor coach to ride in. One
has said that the best thing in the world came out
of Nazareth. But Philip was patient. He only
asked a trial. "Come and see." The claims of
Jesus are not to be settled finally in the realm of
abstract discussion. The argument from experience
is a scientific argument. Philip rested his whole case
right there. He knew what Jesus had done for him.
Nathanael could not refuse to come. So he came to
investigate Jesus, but found that Jesus had already

diagnosed him and pronounced him "an Israelite indeed in whom there is no guile." Thus it is a personal issue between Nathanael and Jesus. "Whence knowest thou me"? It is the first time that Jesus exhibits to men supernatural knowledge. Nathanael's scepticism vanishes before this personal experience. He takes Jesus as the Son of God and the King of Israel. He leaps to the full length and recognizes the divine element in Jesus "the Son of Joseph." Jesus prophesies greater things than these which Nathanael will see, for Jesus is the bond of union between earth and heaven. The angels ascend and descend upon the Son of Man, as Christ calls himself now for the first time. It is significant to note how the chief terms used of Jesus afterwards come to the front right at the beginning. He is the Messiah, the son of Joseph, of Nazareth, the Son of Man, rabbi or teacher, the King of Israel, the Lamb of God, the Son of God.

3. *The First Miracle.*—The devil had tried to get Jesus to work his first miracle for himself. He never wrought miracles for himself simply, though he was and is himself the great Miracle. John the Baptist wrought no miracle, so that we cannot say that a prophet was expected to work miracles as a matter of course. The miracles of Jesus do present difficulty to the modern scientific mind. They cre-

ated difficulty then also, so much so indeed that the
enemies of Jesus attributed them to the devil. But
the modern approach to the subject of miracles is
through the person of Christ. If he was in reality
the Son of God, it is not surprising that he should
exercise the power of God. The remaining difficulty lies in the relation of God to the world. If
God has not exhausted his power in the laws of
nature known to us, we may not limit the expression
of his will. The more real and spiritual God is,
the less reason we have for denying his power in
nature. The suggestion for this miracle came from
the mother of Jesus, and shows that she knew that
he had entered upon his Messianic work and that
she believed in him. And yet, while the suggestion
was perfectly natural and indicates an intimate relation of fellowship between mother and son, a demand was created by it for an outline of the new
situation. The very fact that he had entered upon
his Messianic work made it impossible for Mary
longer to exercise a mother's power over him. Jesus
had no harshness in the use of the word "Woman,"
but it was necessary for her to understand the new
relation. Perhaps his "hour" had not come for a
public demonstration or issue as will come later in
Jerusalem. He did adopt the suggestion of his
mother and change the water into wine, real wine.

Jesus thus had power over nature. His first miracle is as hard as any. He is Lord of nature, and the water recognized that fact and responded to his will.

"The conscious water saw its God and blushed."

Jesus knew how to mingle in social life in such a way as to bless and gladden. He was no recluse who held aloof from men. He lived in the world, but was not tainted by the world. The lover of temperance, as Jesus was, is not driven to false exegesis of this beautiful incident to justify his plea even for local option or prohibition. The light wines of that time were taken with three parts of water and were about like our tea or coffee in effect. Jesus was no advocate of the modern saloon with its traffic in human souls. The glory of Jesus was manifest to the little group of a half dozen disciples who now exercised fresh faith in the new Master. A brief visit to Capernaum with his mother and the band of disciples followed the wedding feast at Cana.

4. *The Issue with the Jerusalem Authorities.*—It was proper that Jesus should go to the feast of the passover. There was no better time for the Messiah to meet the religious leaders of the people than at this great feast. Here first we come to a note of time in the public ministry of Christ, and it is John

who gives it, not the Synoptics. For all that they
tell, the work of Christ might have culminated in a
year, though a crowded one. But John, if we take
his Gospel to be fairly chronological, makes at least
two and a half years with three passovers, with the
possibility of three and a half years. So it was in
the spring of A.D. 27, let us say, that Jesus is in
Jerusalem for the first time since his baptism some
six months before. He is in the temple, where he
loved to be when a boy of twelve, the house of his
Father. Here also he realizes that it is his Father's
house that is desecrated with the barter and sale of
doves and sheep, the clink of money, and the clamor
of the money changers in the corridors of the Court
of the Gentiles. He is not engaged in theological
discussion as before, but this outrage, this graft
which enriches the priestly rulers, so stirred Jesus
that he turns reformer at once and asserts his prophetic and Messianic authority. It is objected that
the Synoptics give this incident at the close of
Christ's ministry and not at the beginning as John
has it. But surely it was of such a nature as to
make it likely to occur again when the tradesmen
returned to their desecration. The influence of
Jesus was only personal and momentary. The
men rallied and wondered what they went out for
anyhow. The Jews demanded a sign in proof of

his claims in doing what only the Messiah had a
right to do. So here at the start the issue is drawn
between Jesus and the ecclesiastical authorities.
He could have wrought a great sign and made verbal
claim to be the Messiah. Would they have accepted
him ? Nay, rather they would have killed him now
instead of three years hence. He does give them
a sign, but one which they do not understand, nor
the disciples. He gave the sign of his death and
resurrection, the great sign on which he staked his
whole career. It was in symbolic and parabolic
form, but for that very reason stuck in the minds of
the people, though with a misunderstanding, as is
shown when at the trial of Christ this misinterpre-
tation is all that the enemies of Jesus can find against
him. And on the cross it will be flung in his teeth
that he had said that he would destroy the temple
and raise it again in three days. He had not said
that. He had said a great deal more. He had
said that, if they destroyed the temple of his body,
he would raise it up in three days. This is not merely
John's interpretation of the parable of Jesus. It is
the only interpretation in harmony with the career
of Christ.

It is objected that it is an anti-climax for Jesus
thus at the start to announce his death, that he
could have no spirit to go on if that was the foreseen

end. But this objection takes too narrow a view of
the career of Jesus and makes his soul too small.
He came to earth at all to die for sinners. He
would not commit suicide. He would let events
work out their course. He would not hasten his
"hour," but would go bravely on to meet it. To
take out from the mind of Christ this early knowledge of his death would rob him of the chief element of transcendent heroism, would make him a
blind groper after the good, rather than the great
constructive spirit who saw that the only hope of the
race was for him to lay down his own life for it. But
in doing so and before doing so he will do a man's
part also. He will attack the evil conditions all
about him in religion and in life. He will set up
the ideal before men, both in word and deed. His
death will rest upon a life worth living, and that
will be to men the appeal of the ages. This is a
conception worthy of Christ, and it is the one given
in the Gospels. He will begin with the house of God.
That calls for cleansing. Even if men with vested
privileges granted or winked at by the rulers profane
the house of God, he will protest. He will protest
even if they come back. He will lift his voice and
his hand against the violators of law and decency.
That hand is lifted yet and scourges every breaker
of law and order.

5. *An Interview with a Jewish Scholar.*—Nicodemus felt drawn to Jesus as one scholar is to another.   Here was a kindred spirit, a man versed in
the deepest things.   But there was more.   The signs
that he wrought in Jerusalem proved to him that
God was with the new teacher.   And yet Jesus was
persona non grata to the Sanhedrin, of which Nicodemus was a member.   Christ was already a man
taboo with the doctors of divinity.   It was partly
due to the fact that Jesus was not a technical
schoolman in their sense, not a graduate of their
rabbinical seminary, had not learned from them;
but partly also to an element of novelty in his teachings.   His standpoint was so unconventional and
so different.   They could not at first place him.
He was unsafe for their theology.   His collision in
the temple accented it all.   The rabbis apprehended trouble.   But all the more Nicodemus was
drawn to him.

We may picture this timid and inquiring scholar
going by night to a tent on the hill outside of the city,
with many a covert glance by the way.   His intro-
ductory remarks pave the way for more intimate
conversation.   Here is a very different man from
either Simon or Nathanael.   He is the inquiring
scholar hedged about by custom and intellectual
abstraction, drawn by truth if only he can see his

way through the maze. Nicodemus is the slave of
the ceremonial system, and does not know it. So
Jesus at once puts before him the heart of the whole
matter, the necessity of the new birth for entrance
into the Kingdom of God. The helplessness of
Nicodemus before that fundamental idea in the
kingdom of grace shows how much he was entangled
in the meshes of legalism. Jesus attempts to help
him by suggesting an advance from his own point
of view. There must be not only ceremonial new
birth, which was easy to Nicodemus, but spiritual
new birth, which is axiomatic with us. "Ye must
be born anew."

Nicodemus had come for light and he had received
more than he knew what to do with, though it was
destined to bring him into the Kingdom. But
Jesus insisted that this was a mere elementary
earthly truth in the Kingdom and not a heavenly
truth that reached back to the eternal purpose
of God as shown in the necessity of the atoning
death of Christ. This "must" took Nicodemus in
too deep, and we still wonder over the depth of love
as set forth in John 3 : 16, whether it is the Evangelist's own interpretation or the closing words of
Jesus to Nicodemus.

The work of Christ in Judea was more successful than that in Jerusalem, though even there more

people believed nominally in Jesus than he could
trust.   In Judea the tide of popularity rose so high
that the jealousy of the Pharisees was aroused.   But
the Baptist did not let jealousy enter his heart when
Jesus passed him in popular favor.   The arrest of
John merely showed what was in store for Christ
when the issue was sharply joined.

   6. *An Interview with a Samaritan Woman.*—It
is hard to put ourselves in the place of Jesus as he
talked with the Samaritan woman by Jacob's well.
Everything was against his endeavoring to win this
one lone woman.   He was worn out with a long
day's mountain travel.   He was hungry.   She was a
woman, and a rabbi was not expected by the Jews
to talk in public with a woman.   She was a Samaritan, whom the Jews hated all the more cordially
because she was half Jew.   She was a woman who
had had too many husbands and whose character
and reputation made a very delicate and difficult case
to handle.   Surely here was a more hopeless proposi-
tion than that of Nicodemus.   Every reason of race
prejudice and personal inclination argued for letting
her alone.   But Jesus never rose to greater heights
than when he roused himself to win this sinful
woman.   He began with a drink of water. the one
common topic between them.   There is no finer
study in the method of soul-winning than in the su-

preme skill shown by Jesus here in overcoming
every obstacle and finally reaching the conscience
of the woman herself. She was eager for theological controversy when she suspected that Jesus was
a prophet. That was her use for a preacher, a dispute. But Jesus held her to the point and revealed to her the highest word that he had to give
about God and worship, and told her plainly that
he was the Messiah, a thing he had not told Nicodemus. The result justified the patient perse-
verance of Jesus, for her conversion led to that of
many others. Jesus saw in the saving of this Samaritan woman the promise of victory. The
harvest of the world was indeed ripe for the sickle
of the reaper when such a woman as this could be
converted. The harvest is still ripe, waiting for
the reapers. But the soul of Jesus fed on this blessed
fruitage. He cared naught for food and water now.
The will of God was enough. He was now becoming the Saviour of the World, for even Samaritans
can be saved.

7. *The Call to Nazareth.*—It is not surprising
that Jesus should wish to visit Nazareth. Indeed,
he made a second visit later, according to the account
in Mark and Matthew. It was only fair to give
Nazareth, the home of his childhood and youth, a
good opportunity. True, Jesus remained away

after his baptism till his ministry was well under
way. He came then with an acquired reputation
as a rabbi, and with even more, for many had heard
of his miracles. But with some there was lingering
doubt how a young carpenter, reared in their town,
whom they knew, could do all the things ascribed
to him. There must be a mistake somewhere, they
felt. But at the start Jesus was treated with every
courtesy. When he read the famous passage in the
roll of Isaiah and gave it back to the attendant,
Jesus sat down by the reading desk. That was the
sign that he was going to make an address, and instantly all eyes were fastened on him. They were
on the *qui vive*, for now they would be able to tell
for themselves what there was in him to justify his
sudden reputation since he had left them.

They had not long to wait, for Jesus claimed the
fulfillment on this day of the Messianic promise
just read. The very boldness of the claim won a
sympathetic hearing at first. Just to think of it!
The Messiah has arisen in our town! Their pride
was aroused, and they fell under the spell of his
wondrous speech. But still, was not this Joseph's
son? Incredulity was expressed in their faces and
perhaps in whispers. It is a mortal offense with
some people for their neighbors and friends to succeed beyond them. The idea of superior gifts and

work is out of the question. It is this underlying resentment that Jesus meets when he interprets it by the parable or proverb, "Physician, heal thyself." They were longing for him to do some of the miracles of which they had heard. After all, talk was easy. Work a miracle or two. Jesus could interpret accurately the psychology of a crowd. But instead of accommodating their idle curiosity, he gave them a stern rebuke, with the example of the sovereignty of God as shown in the case of the widow of Zarephath, and Naaman the Syrian. Nazareth had no natural privileges in the Kingdom above any other town. They took this as a thrust at their town pride, and instantly anger filled them all, so that they attempted the life of the hero of the hour before. It was a sad outcome, but Jesus was not surprised, for he said, "No prophet is acceptable in his own country." It was now clear that Nazareth could not be the centre of the Galilean work. Jesus had been too popular in Judea and so had to cease his work there. But he is not too popular in Nazareth.

8. *The New Home.*—Where should Jesus now make his headquarters? It must be somewhere in Galilee. Judea had become impossible, and Samaria was obviously out of the question. In Galilee no town was more cosmopolitan than Capernaum.

The Pharisees had less influence in Galilee than in
Judea, and here at least was an opportunity of sow-
ing the seed of the Kingdom free from the domi-
nating ecclesiastics of Jerusalem.   The Gentile element in Galilee was still considerable, especially
around the Sea of Galilee, which was the centre of
a large trade.   The outer world pressed upon Capernaum, though the Jews had a synagogue there, the
gift of a generous Roman centurion.   Nazareth
itself was near one of the great caravan routes between Egypt and Syria and Mesopotamia.   Aramaic
and Greek were the languages chiefly heard, both
of which Jesus and the disciples probably spoke according to occasion, as was true of Paul also.

The half dozen disciples who had been with Jesus
in Judea and Samaria seem not to have gone with
him to Nazareth, but rather to their several homes.
Four of them, two pairs of brothers, were back at
their fishing.   When Jesus came to Capernaum to
live, he soon found Andrew and Simon, James and
John.   They had not indeed had any luck on this
occasion, and were mending and washing their nets.
To Simon Jesus suggested that he put out in his
boat and try again.   A fisherman can always try
once more.   But Simon had no further hope.   "But
at thy word I will let down the net."   If it pleased
Jesus, he would try once more, though he had toiled

all night and caught nothing. The result humbled
Simon and enabled Christ to draw a valuable spiritual lesson for Simon and the rest. Will he have
as little faith as a fisher of men? This is the second time these four men follow Christ, though not
yet as Apostles. They continue with him, leaving
their fishing for good.

In the synagogue at Capernaum Jesus is before
a strange audience, though not a hostile one. What
astonished the assembly was the personal independence of Jesus as a teacher. He was not the slave of
the past, as the usual rabbi was who was afraid of a
new opinion that did not have the support of some
learned rabbi of old. But Jesus taught not as the
scribes, but as one having authority. He had the
authority of truth and not the dictum of some self-
appointed custodian of orthodoxy. It had been a
long time since a new idea had been expressed in
this synagogue and it created a commotion. What
the world needs is the truth, whether new or old.
A lie is no more true because hoary with age. A
pulpit should not have the dry rot nor the itch for
the merely new. In this case the truth was a sen-
sation. "What is this? A new teaching?" We
have here also the first incident of many when Jesus
healed a poor demoniac. The demon recognized
Jesus as the Holy One of God, but his testimony

was not welcome for obvious reasons. It would not help Jesus to have such attestation. But the people were amazed at his power to cast the demon out. There are serious difficulties connected with the subject of demons, their reality and their relation to disease. We know too little of the spirit-world and psychic phenomena to be able to deny the reality of demons. If the devil exists, demons may without doubt. Missionaries in China to-day claim to have met similar phenomena in modern times. One is slow to credit Jesus with merely humoring the illusions of the time. The Babylonian and Persian teachings of demons do not prove necessarily that the idea of Jesus was illusion or delusion.

The life at Capernaum was manifestly a busy one. On this very Sabbath Jesus raised Peter's mother-in-law from a fever. Please observe that no protest is made on this Sabbath against the cures wrought on this day. The Pharisees have not yet begun to work against him in Galilee. One of the most beautiful scenes in the life of Jesus is at the close of this day. As the sun was setting, he stood in the door of the house and healed all who passed by. His name and fame filled all the town.

9. *The Lines Drawn in Galilee Also.*—The strain upon Jesus was now very great. We find him rising

a great while before day to secure a quiet place for prayer, and then the multitudes seek him.   Jesus no longer lingers in Capernaum, but makes a tour of most of Galilee, apparently with these four disciples. We have no incidents recorded of his first formal tour of the country, though the healing of the leper may be one.   We must expand the general statements made in the Gospels and imagine the vast amount of work done.   In the case of the leper so much excitement arose that Jesus had to withdraw again to the desert places to pray.   He had strictly charged the man not to tell, but, as often happens, all the more the report spread.

We are told, however, several incidents of this period falling in Capernaum after the return home. One of them is the case of the paralytic let down through the roof because of the press at the door. The significant thing here is that the Pharisees are present, and eager to find fault and make charges against Jesus.   This is the first time that the Pharisees appear in opposition in Galilee.   Christ will no more have a free hand even here.   It is to be observed also that they come not only "out of every village of Galilee," but also "out of Judea and Jerusalem," these "Pharisees and doctors of the law sitting by" (Luke 5 : 17).   The recent tour had stirred up the waters in Galilee, and the local

theologians had evidently appealed to Jerusalem
for help. What was Jesus to do in the midst of so
much traditional orthodoxy? They had already
condemned him in their hearts as guilty of heresy.
Their eyes gleamed with envy and they smiled with
satisfaction, the long-bearded hypocrites! He will
not attempt any hocus-pocus now that we are here,
for we are ready for the impostor! Jesus gave them
a handle at once. He offered the paralytic forgiveness of sins. This rankled in their hearts, for according to their theology no one can forgive sins but
God. Hence Jesus had claimed to be God. But
even so they only felt and looked their indignation.
They were not so brave as they supposed. But
Jesus knew their hearts and accepted the unexpressed
challenge. He bade the paralytic take up his bed
and walk right then and there as a proof of his
power on earth as the Son of Man to forgive sins.
It was audacious. The worst offence of all was that
the palsied man did get up without even asking their
permission! "We never saw it on this fashion,"
the people said. And the Pharisees? They now
feared him, but were the more bent on his ruin. If
let alone he will overturn all Pharisaical theology.
That calamity the world could not survive!

Jesus won a notable disciple when Levi the publican responded to his invitation. The Pharisees

would not have asked him to be their disciple. "Publicans and sinners" were branded together as the
lowest of men. This was worse than to pick up
ignorant fishermen to follow him. Perhaps Levi
was impressed by the very fact that Jesus broke over
social caste and sought him. There was a real man
in this publican, and he instantly went with Jesus.
He was very grateful to the new Teacher and loyal
to his old friends. So he gave Jesus a feast and
asked a great multitude of publicans and other sinners, and Christ accepted. He did not ask the Pharisees, but they went! They would have declined a
formal invitation. They were too pious to associate
with such "trash." It was a custom then for all
who wished to come to the feast and stand by the
wall and watch, if they liked. These pious Pharisees and their scribes (students) did this. They
stood off and made remarks about Jesus while he
enjoyed the feast, a delightful occupation! "He
eats and drinks with publicans and sinners." Jesus
heard their talk and said: "Go ye and learn." This
to the doctors of theology! Yes, go ye and learn
that spirit is more than form with God, though not
with you. Taking the Pharisees at their own estimate of themselves, Jesus had come to heal the sick,
not the well.

Growing out of this dispute comes the discussion

about fasting. Even some of the disciples of John
the Baptist are led by the Pharisees to complain that
the disciples of Jesus do not observe the stated fasts.
They are, therefore, not orthodox. This complaint
gives Christ an opportunity to draw in outline by
three illustrations (bridegroom, new garment, wine-
skin), the vital distinction between Christianity and
Judaism. Christianity is spirit and Judaism is
form. It is impossible to graft Judaism upon
Christianity. The failure to see this nearly wrecked
Christianity in Paul's day, and did ultimately make
a hybrid type of religion dominant through the middle ages, to the lasting injury of the cause of Christ.

For the first time we see Jesus in the chamber of
death. He took only Peter, James, and John, and
the little girl's father and mother. He took her by
the hand and she arose. Death could not stay
where Life was when Life spoke. If this miracle
seems hard to believe, we may remind ourselves
that all are hard to us and all are easy to God.
Jesus was anxious to keep this great deed quiet,
because the envy of the Pharisees had already been
aroused and he foresaw renewed hostility on their
part. So in the case of the two blind men, he charged
that no man know it, but to no effect. The result
was what Christ expected. Already the Pharisees
dare to say, "By the prince of demons casteth he

out demons." They did not deny the cure, but they attributed it to the devil. The demons merely obliged their master.

Jesus is no longer obscure nor unknown. His appeal has been heard all over the land. He is the cynosure of all eyes. But has he won in the rapidly growing struggle with the Pharisees?

CHAPTER III

THE NEW DEPARTURE

"Take my yoke upon you, and learn of me"
(Matt. 11 : 29).

JOHN takes up the narrative again, and we are in Jerusalem at a feast (John 5 : 1). We do not, however, know what feast it is, nor what time of the year Jesus is here. All things considered, we may take it as a passover, though with much reservation and uncertainty. If so, the ministry of Jesus has been going on a year and a half. At any rate, it is the second time that we find Christ in Jerusalem, both occasions being described by John, who gives as a rule the Jerusalem or Judean ministry, while the Synoptics largely present the Galilean work. When Jesus was here before he had a certain popularity with the people, both in the city and in the country. But the rulers were hostile to him. Jesus now comes no more as an unknown rabbi from Nazareth, but as a teacher and miracle worker who has stirred all Galilee. He has a great reputation already.

1. *Conflict over the Sabbath.*—The Pharisees not simply held to the literal and ceremonial regulations

in the Old Testament, but they had added many
more.   Indeed, they had made the day a burden
instead of a blessing.   A large part of Pharisaic religion consisted in seeing to it that other people
carried out to the letter all the pettifogging rules
which they had laid down.   One could hardly turn
around on the Sabbath day without running against
one of the Pharisaic laws.   If a woman looked into
a mirror on the Sabbath, she might see a gray hair
and be tempted to pull it out.   To wear false teeth
on the Sabbath was to carry a burden.   But in the
case of Jesus the Sabbath question was more occasion than cause.   They had long ago decided to
oppose him and his teachings.   In Galilee they
found fault with him for eating with publicans and
sinners, for not making his disciples fast, for assum-
ing to forgive sins and hence for blasphemy, for being
in league with the devil.   Each new link that they
can forge in the chain is welcome.

Jesus was not asked to heal the man by the Pool of
Bethesda.   He was a stranger to the impotent man
who had long waited by the pool for a cure.   It was
the Sabbath day and Jesus took the initiative.
Though the poor man did not know who it was that
told him to get up and walk away with his bed,
the very thing that he could not do, yet he
somehow was impelled to try.   The Jews, who

saw him, cared little about his being healed. That
was a comparatively small matter. The important thing to them was that he was carrying his
bed on the Sabbath. The man felt that he was
guilty and laid the blame on the man who had
healed him—strange gratitude surely. To cap it
all, when he did learn who had healed him, he went
and told the Jews.

Jesus had not courted trouble over the matter,
but he would not run from it. We are not told
what the form of persecution was which they first
used against Jesus, but he defended himself by the
example of the Father. The defense was worse
than the offense. Now they sought to kill him because he made himself equal with God, calling God
his own Father. Jesus did not deny the accusation.
The rather he admitted it and proceeded in the first
formal apology of his person and work that we pos-
sess (John 5 : 19-47) to prove that he is equal with
the Father in all essential things, though he does
nothing contrary to the Father. On the other hand,
he joyfully does the Father's will, and the Father
has set his seal upon him, and will do so to the end.
It was, as we say, throwing down the gauntlet to his
enemies, though they did not take it up. They
did not know exactly how to proceed, for the man
who was healed was a tremendous argument for

Christ. They were no match for him in debate, with all their dialectical subtleties. But the wedge had gone in deeper.

2. *The Battle Renewed in Galilee.*—To the Jerusalem Pharisees Jesus was now a common Sabbath breaker. On his return to Galilee the Pharisees appear again. While going through the wheatfields on the Sabbath, his disciples pluck some of the heads and rub the grain out in their hands. The technical offence to the Pharisees was the rubbing out of the grain. That was work. Instantly the Pharisees make the attack upon the disciples. It is wearisome and pitiful to think of having to deal seriously with such hair-splitters. But Jesus proceeded to defend what his disciples had done by five arguments. He appealed to the historical example of David who ate the shewbread on the Sabbath when in flight. He reminds them that the priests worked in the temple on the Sabbath, and Jesus claims to be greater than the temple. He recalls the message of God in Hosea: "I desire mercy, and not sacrifice." The ceremony counted for nothing with God unless the spiritual worship went along with it, a lesson that scribism had obscured and one that the prophets had great difficulty in enforcing. Besides, man was not made for the Sabbath, but the Sabbath for man, an obvious truth,

but one often hid from view. It is true of the Bible
itself. Men are not saved that there may be some
to obey the Bible, but revelation is given to help
men to come to God. And, to end the whole matter,
Jesus is Lord even of the Sabbath. Jesus observed
the spirit of the Old Testament teaching, but was
not a slave to the mere form. He denied that what
the disciples had done contradicted the real import
of the Old Testament. But even if it did, he claimed
the right to institute a new order of things, for he is
greater than the Sabbath. This point he did not
expand, but in it is contained the germ of the New
Testament attitude towards the day of rest. He
had brushed off his enemies, but left a rankling
sting by his supreme claim concerning the day.

The Sabbath controversy goes on now in various
parts of Palestine to the end, and yet the enemies of
Christ are not able to make out anything against
him serious enough to stand. One difficulty with
the rabbis was that they did not themselves strictly
observe what they so diligently preached to others.
They had Pharisaic orthodoxy, but not Pharisaic
orthopraxy. Hence they could never go to the limit
in the matter. On the very next Sabbath, however,
in a synagogue in Galilee the storm breaks out again.
This time the Pharisees are ready beforehand. They
seemed to know that Jesus would attend this syna-

gogue, and were watching to see if he would dare
heal the poor man with a withered hand who was
there.   Would he do it when they were on hand to
expose him?   They felt their importance keenly,
these regulators of the faith.   But Jesus knew their
thoughts—solemn thought to us—and made a point
of the matter.   He made the man step out where all
could see him.   Then he joined issue with his enemies.   Much depends on the way a thing is put.
Jesus asked if it was right to do good or to do harm
on the Sabbath.   That was unanswerable.   Then
he asked if a man was of more value than a sheep.
This was the crux of the whole question.   They
feared to answer this.   Jesus' eyes flashed with anger
over them as he bade the man to stretch forth his
hand, right before and almost at the Pharisees.   To
the Pharisees this utter rout was unendurable, and
yet what could they do?   They could not keep the
man from stretching out his arm.   There was but
one thing left.   They would kill Jesus.   A man will
never forgive you for giving him an unanswerable
argument.   It is a mortal offence.   They even
counsel with their old enemies, the Herodians,
on the subject, so bitterly do they now hate the
Nazarene.

3. *The New Organization.*—The need of it is now
manifest.   We need not speculate on what was

Christ's plan before this time, nor say that now he
made a radical change in his views.   There is nothing to justify such a statement.   What is clearly
true is that now he can no longer wait for things to
take their course.   There was organized opposition
to Jesus with headquarters in Jerusalem, a regular
conspiracy bent on leaving no stone unturned to
compass his downfall.   Satan is carrying out his
threat with speed.   He has arrayed against Jesus
the religious leaders of the time, the exponents of
the traditional orthodoxy of the day.   The devil
becomes anxious to preserve the harmless faith of
the Pharisees.   He poses as the champion of the
faith.   Jesus is put in the light of an innovator, a
heretic.   If Jesus is to win, he must conquer rabbinical Judaism as well as the powers of the world
of sin.   However much Jesus foresaw all this, there
was inevitable isolation in the result.   He came as
the Messiah of his people, and the accredited teachers of the time shut the door in his face.

Nor is this all.   He had some true believers, but
as yet no organized band of followers, no force
bound to him by hooks of steel.   It was a world-
wide and an age-long conflict.   Steps must be taken
looking towards the future.   Already half of the
public ministry was over.

The purpose of this band is stated in Mark

3:14f. They are to be with Jesus, to preach, and to have authority over demons. This body of preachers was not a local church, nor the church general. It is a special body of men chosen for a special purpose. They are to be charged with the work of starting Christianity upon its world career. They are to be with Jesus till he returns to the Father, so that they may learn Christ and be true exponents of him and his ideas. These men must be teachers of the Kingdom. The policy of Jesus evidently, then, is to teach the teachers. Thus he will guarantee the proper interpretation of his message and mission and the work of the Kingdom of God. It is true that the work of Jesus with these men will need the further teaching of the Holy Spirit, but the foundation on which they will build will be laid by Jesus himself. When this group of men shall be trained by Jesus, he can leave the work to their hands under the guidance of the Holy Spirit. The great Teacher then had a class of twelve to go with him constantly for nearly two years. The choice was made under very solemn circumstances. Jesus had spent a whole night in prayer. It was a crisis, for, humanly speaking, all depended on the choice of these men. He talked with the Father all night about it. In the gray dawn of the morning he came down the mountain side with the dew of heaven on

his brow. A great multitude of believers and of un-
believers was assembled already in the early morning. He seems to have called the men, "whom he
himself would," up to him out of the crowd. Then
he appointed them as Apostles. It was an old term,
but henceforth it was to have with them a new meaning. Afterwards he came down with them to a
level place on the mountain. Here at least is a
nucleus. Will they justify the choice of Jesus?
He had risked his all on them and had chosen them,
as he afterwards said, because he knew them. Some
of them, a majority indeed, had been with him already a good while. The rest Jesus had probably
noticed carefully.

But who are these men? Six of them probably,
Andrew and Simon, James and John, Philip and
Nathanael, became disciples at the beginning at
Bethany, beyond Jordan. Another, Levi, left his
publican's seat some while afterwards. The other
five, James, the son of Alpheus, and Thaddeus,
Thomas, Simon the Cananean, and Judas Iscariot,
meet us here for the first time. They are all of
Galilee save Judas Iscariot, who comes from Judea.
This fact marks him off from the rest at once, but
he seems to have business capacity (though a preach-
er) and soon becomes the treasurer of the band.
There are three groups of brothers, Simon and

Andrew, James and John, James the son of Alpheus
and Judas the brother of James. The four lists that
we have of the twelve were evidently made according to later developments in the group. Simon
Peter always appears first and Judas Iscariot last,
save in Acts when he has dropped out entirely. They
fall into three groups of four, Philip heading the
second, and James the son of Alpheus the third.
Nathanael appears as Bartholomew, and Thaddeus
is also called Judas the brother of James. Simon
the Cananean, or Zelotes, had belonged to the party
of zealots who later brought on the war with the
Romans. Four of them were fishermen. None of
them had theological training until now. With
Jesus they were to be in the greatest school that
earth has ever seen. Aristotle taught Alexander
the Great, but Jesus was the teacher of these men.
They had less to unlearn than if they had been to
Jerusalem to school, but they still shared in the
common theological views of the time. It will be a
task even beyond the power of Christ to lift these
men up to the spiritual interpretation of the Kingdom of God before his death and resurrection.

Did Jesus make a mistake in choosing these men?
Where could he have gotten men better adapted to
his purposes? Not in Jerusalem nor in Judea, and
Judas came out of Judea. They were all men of

ability, as the sequel shows. No rarer spirit has
ever lived than John. Simon Peter was versatile
and alert. Andrew was a man of counsel. Thomas
was cautious. Nathanael (Bartholomew) was a
man free from guile, if a bit sceptical. Levi was a
man of methodical business habits. Simon, the
zealot, had zeal in abundance. James, the brother
of John, was one of the chosen inner circle of three,
and a man to be trusted. Philip seems to be practical and prudent. Of James the Less and his
brother Judas (Thaddeus) we are not able to form
a very clear picture, though we cannot assume that
they were negative characters. Judas once shows a
lack of spiritual insight (John 14 : 22). There was
thus great variety in personal traits, and each had
his strong points. Even Judas Iscariot was not
without special aptitudes, else he would not have
been treasurer (so as to absconding treasurers to-
day who would not have been trusted if they had
not shown capacity). He had his opportunity, poorly
as he used it.

4. *The Declaration of Principles.*—The Sermon
on the Mount has been the occasion of much discussion and even controversy. No other words of
Jesus stand out quite so sharply as these. They
are commonly taken as typical of the mind of Christ.
The ideal of righteousness here set forth is still the

goal of the civilized world in spite of the notion of a few that the teachings of Jesus are wholly out of sympathy with modern life.

The occasion of this discourse seems to have been the choosing of the twelve apostles. Luke so represents the matter, and he is usually chronological. According to Matthew the Sermon stands at the beginning of the Galilean ministry, more as a type of the teaching done by Jesus. But both Matthew and Luke give it as a real discourse at a definite place. They do not differ essentially in the circumstances, for Luke's "plain" need only be a "level place" as the revised version has it, probably a level place on the mountain such as one finds on the Horns of Hattin near Tiberias. From this level place Jesus probably went up on the mountain side a little way and sat down to address the people.

But we are not to think of Jesus as speaking only to the twelve or simply to believers, for both Matthew and Luke mention the presence of the multitudes, Luke indeed recording the fact that they came all the way from Jerusalem to Tyre and Sidon. Many Gentiles were probably on hand, or certainly many Greek-speaking Jews. It is possible, though not certain, that Jesus on this occasion spoke in Greek. But while the discourse was general in its nature and suitable for all, it had a special application to

the twelve and may be compared with the closing
address to them on the night before his death, as
given in John 14 : 17. It is a long journey between
these two occasions. The reality and unity of the
Sermon may therefore be assumed. Matthew has
much more than Luke, but chiefly things that concerned his attitude towards the Jewish teaching.
The reports in Matthew and Luke begin and end
alike and agree in general argument. It is possible,
though not necessarily true, that some of Christ's later
sayings may have been put into this great address.
But it is far more probable that the same or similar
sayings occurring at other points were simply repeated by Jesus on other occasions. Repetition is
not simply allowable; it is necessary for effective
service, especially in the case of a popular teacher
who had to meet different audiences in various parts
of the land. This sermon is admitted by all to have
essential rhetorical unity as reported by Matthew
and Luke. The Sermon on the Mount is a fine example of the teaching of Jesus. The element of
parable is not as pronounced as in some of the later
discourses, but it is here in the case of the two ways,
the two builders, and in numerous figurative allusions.
Here are sharp distinctions drawn, antithesis, invec-
tive, paradox, illustration, precept, warning, appeal.
But one must not make the mistake of supposing

that Jesus has on this occasion said all that he has
to say in condensed form. By no means. Many
great ideas taught by Jesus are not even alluded to
here. Others are merely assumed or implied, as the
new birth, for instance. The disciples were not
yet ready for all Christ had to say, nor will they be
ready for all by the time Jesus comes to die. The
Holy Spirit will take up the teaching and carry it on.
But Christ has laid down a platform of very important principles pertaining to the Kingdom of heaven.
He by no means wishes men to understand that this
is all the teaching that they need, though one can
readily admit that this is enough, and too much for
many. Those who decry theology the most and appeal to the Sermon on the Mount as the sole standard for men are likely to be the very ones who fall
farthest short of the ideal of human life here outlined. This ideal of righteousness is impossible
save to one who has a new heart to begin with and
the help of the Holy Spirit all through to the end.
But this clear-cut epitome of ethical principles made
a pronounced impression then and does to-day soar
above all human ethical standards. The people
wondered at these words, and the world is wondering
still. This is probably not a complete report of the
Sermon, but a brief abstract, the most striking things
that were remembered and told over and over.

There is some difference of opinion as to the theme of the Sermon (as often to-day about sermons), because Luke does not give what we have in Matt. 5 : 17-20. There Christ's Idea of Righteousness seems to be set forth as the theme. And even in Luke this is the implied subject of discussion. It is introduced by the Beatitudes and illustrated and discussed from various points of view. Christ's Idea of Righteousness is to-day the world's Ideal of Righteousness, though one cannot say that the world as yet approximates its ideal. But this much is gained, to have put the goal before the world. At one blow Jesus struck down the standards set up by the scribes and Pharisees. He even said that if his hearers did not do better than that, they had no hope at all. The scribes and Pharisees were the religious leaders of the time. The pity and the pathos of the situation! The boldness of Christ's conceptions is here manifest. He did not compromise nor hesitate. He was laying foundations for all time. He went to the heart of things and saw them as they are. Hence his teaching is universal, pervasive, eternal.

The Beatitudes form the introduction to this great discourse. It is not a new style of speech, occurring often in the Psalms. There are two parts to each Beatitude and special significance in each.

Luke gives only four which are balanced by four woes. The most outstanding thing about the Beatitudes is that Christ's conception of happiness differs so radically from that of the teachers of the time, both Jewish and Greek. The formal ceremonialism of the Pharisees was set at naught by the lofty spirituality here insisted upon. The mere Sadducee would find little to attract him in this transcendental spiritual philosophy. If any Greeks were there, they would be equally puzzled. The Epicurean would prefer the world of sense to this happiness of the spirit. The Stoic would understand the spiritual plea better, but it was all too altruistic for him. All of them had rather do the persecuting than endure it. Vengeance was sweeter to them than mercy, pride than humility, self-conceit than craving to be better. Purity of heart was too inconvenient for a work-a-day world. Only in portions of the Old Testament, especially the Psalms, do we find an approach to this sublime spiritual idealism. The Beatitudes imply a new heart or regeneration. The Kingdom of heaven belongs to those who rejoice in these qualities. In truth no one else will rejoice in them. It should never be forgotten that the possession of the spiritual renewal lies at the basis of Christ's idea of righteousness. It is impossible to all others. It is mere mechanical imitation to seek to reach this ideal without beginning with the foundation laid by Jesus. The Kingdom of God comes before the righteousness. "Seek first the Kingdom of God and his righteousness."

The ideal of righteousness is unfolded from various points of view. It must exceed the standard of the scribes, the accepted teachers of the time among the Jews. These scribes taught the Old Testament plus their own interpretation of it, a second Bible covering up the first. One specimen of that teaching is here condemned by Jesus, "and hate thine enemy" (Matt. 5 : 43). But it is not enough to seek mere formal obedience to the Old Testament. Revelation is progressive. Jesus does not set aside the Old Testament teaching on these points as wrong. It is merely inadequate for the new time. He carries the teaching further in the same direction, from letter to spirit, as illustrated by murder, adultery, oaths, retaliation, enemies. His own words here are not to be pressed literally at all points. He used paradox and even hyperbole to make an impression. But his point is plain. In fact, the ideal of Christ's teaching is the Father. "Ye therefore shall be perfect as your heavenly Father is perfect" (Matt. 5 : 48). Mere labored conformity to this or that detail will not answer.

Nor is the practical righteousness of the Pharisees

one whit better than this unsound teaching of the
traditionalists.   It was vitiated by a grievous fault,
that of self-consciousness.   Alms, prayer, fasting,
were all done to be seen of men.   Missing that, all
was lost to the Pharisee.   Virtue to him was not its
own reward.   A man must be known to give alms.
If necessary, sound a trumpet before you, so as to
attract a crowd and be seen!   The model prayer of
Jesus brings all life into relation to the Father and
puts his Kingdom first.   It is not original in many
of its phrases.   How could a model prayer be wholly
original?

The warning against worldliness hits a sensitive
place.   Trust in God may be all very well, but the
worldly-wise had rather keep one eye on the main
chance.   But the good eye is when both eyes focus
on the same point.   It is not forethought that Jesus
here condemns, but anxiety.   It is not work, but
worry that wears out the machinery of life.   It is
always a sign that something is the matter when the
machine makes too much noise.   The birds sing
as they take what God sends.   Most men assume
that they are themselves right.   Hence they have the
privilege of passing judgment on others.   It is second
nature, if not first.   It is easier to see the mote in
the brother's eye than the big beam in one's own.
Jesus does not mean that we shall not form opinions

about people.   That cannot be helped.   He does
mean that we shall not be hasty, captious, nor unjust in our criticisms.   The habit of criticism is
very vicious.   One can so easily be snappish and
disagreeable.

The Golden Rule is not original with Jesus,
though he first put it so crisply in the positive form.
The practice of it is the original thing with Jesus.
The man who says that this is his religion has some
justification in theory, for Jesus said that it is the
law and the prophets.   Clearly, however, Jesus
meant that this was the sum of the law and the
prophets as they bore upon our relations with our
fellows.   If it be extended toward God, everything
would be included with no reservations.   However, a word of caution is needed to one who is so
easily satisfied.   This inclusive principle of life is
the very hardest one to live up to.   It means far
more than mere good-natured well-wishing for
everybody and everything.   It is the *practice* of
love towards God and man in the widest sense.   It
is more than mere abstinence from harm to our
neighbors.   It is to be an exponent of every positive
grace and virtue.

The narrow gate and the broad way are favorite
images in ethical teaching.   The idea is in Psalm 1.
It appears in the Two Ways, in Barnabas, etc.   It

is an obvious parable of life. It is the straitened,
not necessarily the straight, way. The supreme
test is that of life. Character, not profession, is the
element that endures the crucible of this examination. Many will glibly *say* then who are not willing
to *do* now. Excuses and explanations are always
handy, and mere talk is very easy. One is not to
imagine that Jesus has changed his theology by this
demand that the tree be judged by its fruits. If the
Kingdom of heaven with the new birth lies at the
basis of Christ's idea of righteousness, the man
whose house stands because built upon the rock
pictures graphically the consummation of that righteousness. The good tree does bear some good fruit.
There is a note of confidence as well as of warning
here. Jesus differs from all other ethical teachers
in just this. He gives the power to put into practice
these ethical ideals. It is just because the Kingdom
is in a man that he can finally reach Christ's ideal.
He can and he will. The final and supreme test
of the seed is the fruit. The man whose perfected
life conforms to the great ideal is indubitably one
whose heart was renewed by the spirit of God.
Here, then, is a vital system of ethics. It is righteousness applied to life, and that bears fruit. The
teaching is no longer in the clouds, but is brought
down to men. No wonder that the people were

astonished at such words. It was the glint of the
sunshine through the clouds and fog of rabbinism.
Jesus actually had ideas of his own and spoke with
the authority of transparent truth, not the mechanical
repetition of former rabbis. His words still challenge
our admiration and appeal to our highest selves. To
be what Jesus here commends is to be the noblest
type of man that was ever presented to the world,
for the conscience of Jesus has become the delicate
standard for all the world. His condemnation leaves
no further appeal.

5. *The Despair of John the Baptist.*—At the very
time that Jesus was planning for an aggressive campaign with some organization, John the Baptist was
languishing in the prison at Machaerus. His friends
were allowed to see him, but it was a dreary life, so
utterly different from the wild freedom of the wilderness and the favor of the great multitudes. After
all the excitement to come to this dark solitude
was too much even for a robust nature like John's.
Doubts would come even about Jesus whom he had
baptized and identified as the Messiah. Logic in a
cell and out by the Jordan is not the same thing.
If Jesus was the Messiah, why was he so slow in
setting up the Kingdom? Why did he let John stay
in prison? Perhaps after all there was some mistake.
Maybe Jesus was only another forerunner like him-

self, and the real Messiah was still to come. Reports of the work of Jesus came to John occasionally. Probably the account of the raising of the son of the widow of Nain reached him and quickened his depressed spirit into fresh interest. So he sent two of his disciples with the pathetic appeal to Jesus for more light. Jesus was busy at the time with his cures and kept on till he was done. Then he bade these two disciples to go tell John what they had seen and heard. He added a beatitude to the effect that he was blessed who found no occasion of stumbling in him—a gentle rebuke to John. Jesus was not without sympathy for John at such a time, but the most effective reply was work, not words. He was doing the work of the Messiah. Jesus treated this request from John seriously. There is nothing to indicate that it was mere make-believe on John's part. If we wonder that John could fall into doubt, let us recall the case of Elijah, the prototype of John, and even the mother of Jesus later. After all, Jesus was not the conventional Messiah, and hid in the dark as John now was he could easily go astray.

But Jesus took occasion to pass a wonderful tribute upon John, one that would have cheered him greatly could he have heard of it. He recalls the multitudes who flocked to the wilderness to see, not

a reed shaken in the wind, not an effeminate man of
the city, but a son of the soil, a prophet and more,
a man as great as any born of woman, an epoch-
making man who divided the past from the future.
He was the close of the old age and the beginning of
the new, so that in one sense all those in the new
have an advantage over him. He is Elijah that was
to come. True, he was not accepted by all men,
as Jesus was not. The Pharisees and Sadducees
rejected his baptism, while the masses and even the
publicans justified and glorified God because of
John. To the leaders John was too much of an
ascetic. He was peculiar, different from other folks.
His dress, his diet, his home all marked him from
men. But to the same men Jesus was equally ob-
jectionable. He did live with men, ate their food,
lived in their homes. They called him therefore a
wine-bibber and a glutton, a palpable falsehood.
But they had to find fault with him somewhere.
They said he was too much like other people for a
rabbi! So it goes. What is a preacher to do?
How can he please the people? It is doubtful if he
can succeed, and he ought not to succeed if he makes
merely that his aim. The best that one can do is
to do right and let the results speak for themselves.
Wisdom is justified in the end by her children (or
works). In the long run the man wins who goes

straight ahead and does his duty.   It was not long
now before Herod yielded to the wiles of his wife
Herodias and was caught in her trap to kill
John.   She had never forgiven him for rebuking
her.   She held it against him (ἐνεῖχεν αὐτῷ).   The
disciples of John "went and told Jesus." He would
understand.

6. *The Son's Relation to the Father.*—In this great
crisis of his career Jesus is fully conscious that the
Father is with him.   In Matt. 11 : 25-30 we have a
section that is identical in tone and point of view
and even in style with the Gospel of John.   Chorazin,
Bethsaida, Capernaum will reject him and be pun-
ished, but Jesus sees victory in the future.   All
things have been delivered into his hands by the
Father.   No one really knows him but the Father,
as no one really knows the Father but the Son.
The way to the Father depends on the will of the
Son, a marvellous claim of elective power.   On the
basis of that power he extends the most gracious invitation to the weary and heavy-laden.   He invites
all to come to school to him and promises that his
yoke will be easy and his burden light.   The twelve
Apostles are already in his school.   He asks for more
pupils who are willing to learn of one who, though
the Son of God with all knowledge and power, is
yet meek and lowly in heart.   Who can refuse to

learn from such a Teacher whose words linger in
the mind like sweet bells at eventide? No teacher
ever made such an offer as Jesus does here. He
will indeed put us under the yoke, but the yoke is,
after all, easy and the burden grows light.

CHAPTER IV

THE GALILEAN CAMPAIGN OR THE REJECTION OF A SPIRITUAL KINGDOM

"Would ye also go away?" (John 6 : 67).

JESUS will now endeavor by vigorous work to win a foothold for the Kingdom in Galilee. He has already preached much in various parts of the country, but the results have not been large. The crowds are great and excitement is intense.

1. *He Makes a Second Tour of Galilee,* taking the twelve with him, his new band of disciples. It will be an experience of much value to them. Certain women, a noble band of workers, followed also during this preaching tour. How early the women began to work for Jesus, and how faithfully they have served him! A church is never better than its women, and not always as good. These good women ministered of their substance for the support of Christ and his company. Perhaps Judas later was influenced by this fact when he resented Mary of Bethany's spending so much money for the ointment, though he spoke of the poor at the time Mary Magdalen was one of this band, and is now

mentioned for the first time. She is not the woman
that was a sinner who at the Pharisee's feast washed
the feet of Jesus. That legend is an unpardonable
slander on Mary Magdalen. Nor was Mary Magdalen the same woman as Mary of Bethany, the sister
of Lazarus. We know nothing of this journey save
the general statements made, but we can easily
imagine the character of the work done.

2. *Jesus Repels the Attacks of His Enemies.*—He
has a new cross to bear, that of misunderstanding at
home. His mother and his brethren have become
puzzled over all this stir and confusion. The crowds
are so great that they fail to eat. The family con-
clude that he is beside himself and come to take him
home. He has gone crazy! Poor Mary! It must
have been a sad hour for her. Even John the Baptist had doubted, and now his mother has given up
hope about him. It has all turned out so differ-
ently from the way that she expected the Messiah
would do. He was still just a mere preacher, with
great crowds, it is true, but he was not now claiming
in so many words to be the Messiah. Mary doubtless heard this explanation of Jesus' conduct from
some of her friends who wanted to put the best face
possible on the situation. Our "friends" sometimes
are excessively kind in explaining our conduct.
The people were all seeking to explain the career

of Jesus, while he studiously avoided saying anything that would give his enemies a handle. So the mystery about him grew and deepened.

But the Pharisees were not so charitable in the construction that they put upon the matter. They had already hinted at their view. One day when the multitudes in their amazement went so far as to ask, Is this the Son of David? the Pharisees retorted that he was in league with Beelzebub, the prince of demons! That is the true explanation of his miracles, they said. It was a shock to the multitude and was a public attack right in the presence of Jesus which could not be passed by. They were at some distance from him, but he knew their thoughts and called them to him. They had made a bold shot and a desperate one. Jesus claimed to be the servant of God; in reality he was the agent of Beelzebub. The issue was fairly joined. Jesus replied with a string of sententious aphorisms (parables) that cut to the quick. He points out the absurdity of their charge, for Satan would be casting out Satan, a thing he would never do. He uses the *argumentum ad hominem* on them. They claimed also to cast out demons. By whom did they do it? It was a fair turn. Jesus could use this weapon without committing himself to the reality of their claim. Here is a *reductio ad absurdum*. Christ then presses the alternative that he cast out demons by the spirit of God rather than by the devil. The conclusion is that the Kingdom of God has come upon them. It was a complete turning of the tables, but Jesus is not done yet. They have themselves committed the unpardonable sin of attributing the manifest work of the Spirit of God to the power of the devil. That was inexcusable and would never be forgiven. They were guilty of an eternal sin. It was more excusable if one blasphemed Jesus, who was man as well as God. He was the Son of Man. Even now Christ is not through with his arraignment. With something of the fire of John the Baptist and of his own later denunciation of his enemies (Matt. 23), he turns upon them and calls them "offspring of vipers." They are evil and can only speak evil.

One would have thought that the Pharisees would have withered away under this righteous denunciation. But some of them blandly stepped up and asked that Jesus work a sign! They probably meant it in ridicule, but they got still more denunciation. Christ calls them "an evil and adulterous generation." They repeat the usual Jewish idea of the Messiah, that he will come with spectacular display. Jesus gives them the sign of his death and resurrection, with a reference to the story of Jonah. The sign of Jonah was, of course, lost upon them, though Jesus expressly said that the Son of Man should be three days and three nights in the heart of the earth, *i. e.*, three days as men count days, not meaning to accent unduly night from day. He reminds them how the men of Nineveh repented at the preaching of Jonah, a thing which they were not doing.

The mother and brethren of Jesus press up to the house to have a word with him and take him home. Jesus "looked round on them which sat round about him" and said: "Behold, my mother and my brethren." He was no longer to be commanded even by his mother. He had entered a larger fellowship of the Spirit to which he admitted every one who did the will of God. His disciples were his real kindred, for at this moment those bound to him by the ties of the flesh had failed to understand him. Mary, though so close to Jesus, just now had lost her way. But she will find it again and some day even his brothers will believe.

3. *Jesus Adopts a New Style of Teaching.*—It is not the first time that Jesus used parables, but the first time that he had made a point of doing so. Those used theretofore had been brief and isolated. On this occasion they are many and at much length. But from now on they form a marked characteristic of his teaching and make a definite turn in his method

of instruction. Jesus will bear the closest scrutiny
as a teacher who followed the deepest laws of nature
in his efforts to reach the hearts of men, followed
them naturally and almost artlessly, while we blunder
on and painfully discover some of the great principles of teaching.   It is one of the hopeful signs of
modern times that we are seeing the importance of
studying the pupil as well as the subject to be taught.
Jesus in this very context urged his hearers to take
heed what they heard and how they heard.

The parable is not an invention of Jesus.   The
Jewish rabbis were fond of using this form of instruction.   There is nothing to prevent any modern
teacher from using the parable, and some do.   But
the parables of Jesus so far surpass those of all other
men that the rest sink away into oblivion.   His parables ring clear and true and perfect.   They are not
overdone nor underdone.   They illustrate rather
than darken the point.   This is by no means the
least noteworthy fact.   The term parable is used in
a variety of ways, but the essential idea is that of
an objective parallel to moral or spiritual truth
($\pi\alpha\rho\alpha\beta o\lambda\acute{\eta}$).   On this occasion, as usual, the
parables of Jesus grew out of the circumstances.
The hostile attitude of friends and enemies on his
busy day gave the tone to this entire group.   They
had accused him of being in league with the devil.

Hence they did not deserve to receive more of the teaching of Jesus. The use of parables now served to hide the mysteries of the Kingdom from his enemies, while the spiritually minded would remember the wonderful story and by and by understand the teaching contained in it. The harshness of this judgment upon the enemies of Christ is much relieved when the actual circumstances of this day are perceived. The day will come when the Pharisees will see the point of those parables directed against them.

It is no wonder that Jesus wished to get out of the stuffy hostile atmosphere of the house and into the bracing air of beautiful Galilee. But even here he found a crowd and sat down in the boat and taught the multitudes on the shore. The people were astonished as he taught them in parables, and even the disciples could not understand him. We are such slaves to routine and intellectual ritual that the new gives us a jolt. We do not know how many parables Jesus spoke on this day. Matthew gives seven and Mark one more, but he spoke "many such parables," it is added. Things new and old Jesus brought out of his store. Some were spoken after he left the shore and went back to the house. Two of them (the Sower and the Tares) were explained by Jesus at the request of the disciples. They serve as models for the interpretation of the parables that are not explained.

The eight that are preserved for us from this day's teaching fall into four pairs: the Sower and the Seed, the Tares and the Net, the Leaven and Mustard Seed, the Hid Treasure and the Pearl of Great Price. They illustrate together many sides of the Kingdom of heaven, which is indeed like a diamond with numerous facets; and again the Kingdom of God is a vital growth and cannot be analyzed, as life refuses to be put under the microscope. The Kingdom of God has various results due to the diversity of soil, and the secret of its growth in the heart is like that of nature. The line of cleavage between those who have the Kingdom and those who have not is not made perfectly clear as yet. They grow in the same field (the world) till the harvest time. The growth of the Kingdom, while slow and from small beginnings, is sure and pervasive. It will ultimately cover the earth. Meanwhile, spite of much evil and discouragement, many will find joy in the Kingdom and consider it the greatest treasure of earth. There will be other great groups of parables, but none will surpass in suggestiveness this first one.

4. *Jesus in Heathen Territory.*—It had been a day of stress and storm, the sample of many in the life of Jesus. The wedge had entered deeper and the

cleft was wider between Jesus and the rulers.   The
iron had indeed entered the soul of Christ.   With a
heavy heart and a weary body he sank down into
the stern of the boat "even as he was" and pushed
out with the disciples at eventide to cross over the
lake.   Perhaps the wind and the waves would bring
rest.   No wonder that Jesus was soon asleep.
When the sudden squall from the north fell down
upon the little lake and tossed the water into fury,
Jesus slept on till the excited disciples awoke him
with a cry of despair.   He spoke to the wind and the
sea and they obeyed him; they did, though the Pharisees had just reviled him.   The disciples marvel as
to what manner of man he is.   They had taken him
to be the Messiah, but it was not perfectly clear to
their minds what the Messiah would be.   They
grew in perception of the content of the term Messiah to the end of their career.   There was, therefore, a twofold development.   Jesus revealed himself more and more to the disciples, and they grew
in apprehension of him.   On the shore the Master
had an experience of horror.   It was in the region
of Decapolis at the village of Khersa (Gerasa) not
far from Gadara.   The wild demoniac rushing along
among the rocks was not a sight to give rest of spirit.
And even the sea had turned to storm.   But at least
Jesus gave peace of heart to this unfortunate man.

The mystery of the demoniacal possessions never appears darker than in this incident. The destruction of the swine added to the ravings of the man make a dreadful background in the twilight on this heathen shore. The mystery of evil is not relieved by the denial of the devil and demons. The presence of disease here may or may not be in conjunction with the power of the evil one. The assumption that Jesus was merely accommodating himself to custom in speaking of demons cannot solve all the difficulties concerning the demon possession. As previously said, we know too little about psychic matters to say the final word here. But let us at least rejoice that Jesus is master over both sin and disease. He will sometimes bless those who do not appreciate it. The people of the community begged Jesus to leave their shores for good, but the picture of the man, once so wild, sitting clothed, in his right mind is a comfort to those who battle with sin in country or in city. Here, where no Pharisees are to molest, Jesus tells the man to go to his house and tell what great things God has done for him.

5. *Jesus Makes a Last Visit to Nazareth.*—Nazareth did not deserve this second opportunity. Some scholars indeed deny that it was so, but on the whole it seems probable that this is not the early visit recorded by Luke. It is not surprising that

Jesus should once more come to Nazareth, the home
of his childhood, in spite of the treatment received
the last time. It was his own country. True
enough, as he finds, a prophet has no honor, no lasting honor, in his own country, among his own kin,
and in his own house. But he would give them their
chance. They are astonished. They are incredulous.
How can it be? Where did it all come from? We
know his family and we know him. They stumbled
at him and even refused to believe what they saw
with their own eyes. In such a sceptical atmosphere Jesus did few mighty deeds. So great in fact
was their unbelief that he marvelled at it. And this
at Nazareth. It must have been a sad look that Jesus
gave Nazareth as he saw it for the last time and passed
over the hill and out of sight. Who will welcome
Jesus now? The heathen region of Decapolis had
turned him away. His own home had pushed him
aside. Jerusalem was bent on his destruction.
Will Galilee endure him, when she knows the truth?

6. *A Third Tour of Galilee.*—This tour will settle
the matter so far as Galilee is concerned. It will be
the last. The occasion was the compassion of Jesus
for the multitudes. He had indeed a little band of
laborers, but they were utterly unable to cope with
the situation in Galilee. The harvest was great and
the laborers few. The remedy suggested by Christ

for this new recruiting dilemma is prayer to the
Lord of the Harvest. Somehow we fail to em-
phasize the one item laid upon preachers by Jesus,
that they pray for other preachers to be raised up.
There can be no jealousy here, for it is a world
need.

But these twelve must go and reap what they can.
So Jesus sends them forth for the first time without
him. They have had much instruction and obser-
vation. Now they can put it into practice. It is
one thing to study about preaching. It is quite another thing to preach. Will they succeed as they go
and preach the Kingdom of God? Will sinners be
converted under their preaching? Will the demons
go out at their command? Who does not recall his
first experience in leading a soul to Christ? The
Master will follow them to see how their work turns
out, for much depends on these men. In the struggle with the Jerusalem authorities they had the power
and prestige of State and the strength of prejudice.
What if the disciples fail utterly after all their training?

Jesus renews his instructions to them, or rather
gives them in condensed form the main ideas that
they will need for this tour, incidental details as well
as fundamental principles. Some of the things here
enjoined were afterwards expressly changed by

Jesus, as the direction not to go in the way of the Gentiles or the Samaritans. The "Hardshell" spirit has always made a literal interpretation of the words of Jesus on this point, but with blind obscuring of the historical situation and the later commands of the Master. But let no one think that common-sense details as to food, clothing, manners have little value. They go largely to determine the ultimate success of every minister.

The point that Jesus laid most stress on was the spirit with which they should go. They go forth as sheep in the midst of wolves, a vivid picture of helplessness. But they are not to fear the wolves. If they are persecuted in one city, they will go on to the next. The one to fear is God, not man. After all, Jesus came to send a sword, not peace. This seems like a flat contradiction of what Christ had said elsewhere. But we must put together all that he said, however paradoxical it may appear. Then the result will be clear. The man who cringes with fear to save his life from the wolves will lose his life. This is the paradox of courage and sacrifice, but it is the law of life. Along with dove-like innocence, they are to have the wisdom of serpents. It is the combination that Jesus commands, not the isolated possession of either quality. So the new preachers of the gospel went forth into all Galilee. They did cast out many demons and preached the gospel of the Kingdom.

The dread of Herod Antipas was one result. The disciples manifested due courage and achieved some degree of success. Galilee was apparently stirred to the foundation by this concerted campaign. News of the commotion reached Herod Antipas who was already the victim of his fears. He had never felt right about the death of John the Baptist, and was anxious to see if it was not John come to life again. Others thought Jesus was Elijah or another of the prophets. But Jesus studiously kept out of the way of Herod, a name that boded no good to him.

7. *Will the Galileans Accept a Spiritual Messiah?* —As yet they do not fully understand what Jesus claims to be. They know him as a wonderful teacher, a worker of miracles, a man who has won the enmity of the ecclesiastical forces in Jerusalem, who is reviled by the Pharisees in Galilee, but who is immensely popular with the people. He had not said to them that he was the Messiah. Who is he?

Great as was the favor in which Jesus was held by the people, the feeding of the five thousand men, besides women and children, carried the enthusiasm beyond all bounds. Christ and the disciples had just returned from the great tour of Galilee and were

seeking the hillsides near Bethsaida Julias for rest.
But a great host of people awaited him there.
They lined the mountain eager for his words and
his works.   Jesus stood out in full view of all who
had come.   His heart was tender towards the multitude.   He taught them, and he did more.   He offered
to feed the entire host with a few loaves and fishes
from a lad who was there.   It was a glorious scene
as with their colored garments they reclined in rows
like garden beds on the green grass.   They saw the
constant dispensing of fish and loaves from the
hands of Jesus, and, what was more, they ate them.
There was but one conclusion.   He was the Messiah.
We will take him to Jerusalem and make him King.
No matter what the Pharisees think.   We know
that Jesus is the Messiah.   We will set up the Messianic reign in Jerusalem and drive out the hated
Romans and win the world for the Jews.   That was
the Messianic hope of the Pharisees.   It was the
voice of the people, but not the voice of God.   The
voice of the people is *vox dei* if it is not *vox diaboli*.
This time it was the same temptation that Satan had
offered Jesus in the beginning.   Christ saw that he
must act quickly.   So he dismissed the people to
their homes and sent the disciples back in the boat.
He himself went up into the mountain to talk with
the Father who alone would understand him and his

loneliness. There he found the sympathy that he needed. He won his victory again over this fresh temptation, but he lost the Galileans as we shall soon see. To the disciples Jesus at first seemed like a spectre as they see him gliding over the water towards them. Peter was bold enough to wish to walk on the water with him till he saw the wind coming and his heart sank, and so did he. In the boat the disciples worship Jesus as the Son of God.

Christ was now at the height of favor with the Galileans. He was the man of the hour with the people; yes, the man of the hour. Was he the man of all time with them? Jesus was determined to let the multitude know his true character. They labored under a misapprehension. He will not employ terms to give his enemies a club to use on him, but the Galileans must know that he does not claim to be a temporal Messiah. He has not come to fulfill their political dreams. He has come to give them eternal life, a far greater blessing, if they only knew it. So Jesus makes a point of coming over to the synagogue the next morning in order to tell the people the truth. He would like to have their love and loyalty, but on proper terms. The Master bluntly told them that all they wished was to get the loaves and fishes. Step by step he seeks to lead them on to wish for the meat that abides to eternal life, to eat the true bread of God, which is Jesus himself, to take him as the bread of life, in a word to "eat" him. A perfect storm at last broke loose in the synagogue when it dawned on the people that he claimed to have come down from heaven and to be himself the bread of eternal life. Their rage was assisted by keen scepticism which scouted his claims and the possibility of eating him. These rationalists finally wrangled with each other and strode out in disgust. One thing was now certain. Jesus had deliberately broken his hold on a large part of the Galilean populace. He was no longer a popular idol with them.

But the matter did not stop here. Christ had in the audience of professed disciples those who found this a hard saying, especially hard now that so many had gotten up and gone out. Their theological difficulties increased till they too began to leave. People go in herds. They, too, stalked out. Finally all had left Jesus save the twelve. This then was the outcome in Capernaum when the people began to understand what Jesus really claimed to be. If that is the kind of a Messiah that he is, we do not want him! The campaign in Galilee has definitely failed. Christ had no sure foothold in Judea nor Samaria. It is only one year now till the end. He has labored probably two and a half years, and almost nothing is the spiritual result. He knew

crowds, but it saddened Christ when under the fatal
test this assemblage melted away.

Jesus turned to the twelve. What will they do?
It was a solemn moment in his ministry. Once
more all hinged on them. Had they, too, succumbed
to the outgoing tide? They were still here in the
house, but did they wish to go? Were they loyal
yet in heart to Christ? "Would ye also go away?"
Simon is the speaker. His reply indicates that they
had considered going. How could they help it?
But they had decided to stay with him. For one
thing, to whom should they go? There was no hope
back with the Pharisees. Besides, they have a settled trust and experimental knowledge that he is
the Holy One of God. It is not a new experience
with them. They have had it from the first, but
with varying lights and shadows over this blessed
hope. Now, as he has told most about himself,
they are drawn most to him. They would come
closer and learn more. This then is the joy of Jesus.
He has these men at any rate. But even one of
them is a devil.

8. *The Jerusalem Pharisees Renew their Attack.*—
It was an opportune time after the breach between
Jesus and the populace in Capernaum. So the
regulating committee from Jerusalem boldly challenge the orthodoxy of Jesus on the question of eat-

ing with unwashed hands. His disciples had been found guilty of this heinous crime. To their minds it brought up the whole question of ceremonial religion. The disciples of Jesus had transgressed the tradition of the elders. They did not say, but assumed, that this was also the command of God. Now right here is where they missed it. Jesus did not object to washing the hands before meals. That was a good and a proper thing to do. What he did object to was making a doctrine out of this very proper custom, a doctrine on a par with fundamental spiritual matters.

With keen irony the Master exposed the hypocrisy of these champions of ceremonial orthodoxy who violated with impunity the command of God and bound upon others the tradition of men, who knew how to get the credit for punctilious observance of these traditions without the trouble and privation of strictly keeping them, whose orthodoxy consisted in seeing that other people obeyed them, and not in observing them themselves. You make void the word of God by your tradition "and many such things ye do." This sword cut through the armor of self-righteous complacency with which they had approached Christ. They would even wink at robbery of father and mother under the traditional use of "Corban," especially if part of the money came their way.

Jesus was not content with this terrible exposure and arraignment, for he felt that the whole case between him and the Pharisees was summed up in this motto, a spiritual religion versus ceremonialism. He called the multitudes to him and warned them specifically on the point. It was not external observance that made a man good or bad, but the state of the heart. Jesus here laid the axe at the root of the tree of the current Judaism. It was a conflict, in a word, between spiritual truth and mere traditionalism. So strongly had Jesus spoken that the disciples grew uneasy. In the house they ventured to ask Christ if he had not noticed that the Pharisees were made to stumble at what he had said. They still cherished a wholesome dread of the power of the Pharisees. They were afraid that the Master had gone too far. But Christ had no notion of retracing his steps along that line. He saw that it was impossible for him to coöperate with these sticklers for the p's and q's of mere religious observance to the neglect of the spiritual life. "Let them alone: they are blind guides." This is the pathetic description of the Pharisees in the reply of Jesus. They pose as religious lights to point others to the truth, when they themselves are blind and are merely stumbling around in the dark. Luckless travellers are those who follow such spiritual guides. Peter even insisted that Christ explain this parabolic description of the Pharisees, and received a rebuke from Jesus for his dullness in not understanding what he had said about the difference between the spiritual and the ceremonial. In plain terms he tells Peter that out of the heart come forth all evil thoughts and deeds. This lesson, so difficult of apprehension then, is a commonplace now with all evangelical Christians. But even yet the majority of those who name the name of Christ have bound themselves to the externals, to the obscuring or even the destruction of the spiritual realities.

Mark adds that in saying this Jesus made all meats clean. It was, indeed, a revolutionary position to take from the point of view of the average Jew, not to say Pharisee. It is, perhaps, not strange that the disciples themselves stumbled at it. It is worth noting that Peter is the one who will receive the vision on the housetop of Simon the tanner when he will be invited to eat all kinds of meats. The stoutness of his protest then will show how far he is here from fully comprehending all that Jesus had in mind when he spoke. But the seed has been sown that will bear fruit. However, the first result of this conflict was to sharpen the issues between Christ and the Pharisees. They have one more definite ground of complaint against him. The struggle for spiritual religion will not be won in a day, has not indeed been fully won yet in all parts of Christendom. But Jesus is clear that the path of duty lies straight ahead. He has, however, reached a real crisis in his ministry. Evidences multiply that his effective work in Galilee is over. More and more his hopes centre in the twelve. To them he must devote himself more exclusively if they are to be qualified to carry on the work without him and to meet the crucial events now rapidly coming on. Are they now ready for the gloom of his death? It is less than a year to that awful event.

CHAPTER V

THE SPECIAL TRAINING OF THE TWELVE

"But who say ye that I am?" (Matt. 16 : 15).

1. *The Reasons for Such Training Are Obvious.*—It is now less than a year till the end will come. For nearly six months Jesus will devote himself chiefly to the chosen band of men whom he has gathered around him. If these men come to understand him it will not matter so greatly about the rest. As yet they do not fully appreciate either the Messiah or his message. It is supremely difficult for one to rise above his environment. One's standpoint has much to do with what he sees. One of the greatest proofs that Jesus is more than man is just this, that in an environment of cold ceremonialism and external punctiliousness he came with abundant life and spiritual power. So far Jesus has sought to teach mainly the great ideas concerning the Kingdom. He had indeed, in a vital way, outlined the theology of the Kingdom. The disciples did not now understand all that they had heard, nor would they till later. But meanwhile it was necessary that they should learn more of the Messiah himself. Hence-

forth Jesus will speak more concerning the King and less concerning the Kingdom. This is not a wrong historical order, but the right one. The early Messianic disclosures were personal and they largely ceased for obvious reasons. On the broad foundation of the Kingdom teaching Jesus had built, till now they ought to be able, however far the people fell short, to rise to the true idea of the Messiah. The disciples had to expand before he could tell more. But now he must tell more. The time had come when he could not wait longer. The shadow of the cross was coming rapidly towards him. The total eclipse would find the twelve wholly unprepared for the catastrophe. It is not certain that even now the disciples are capable of appreciating all that Jesus has to say about himself and his mission. They have shown signs of development of late which are encouraging. At any rate they must be told the truth.

Jesus sees that it will be difficult to devote himself so exclusively to the disciples in Capernaum or in Galilee. The distractions are too many and the interruptions too frequent in the midst of the excited multitudes. Besides the tension is acute now in Capernaum since the crisis in the synagogue. The issue will be sharper and the lines more tightly drawn between him and the Pharisees. There is

danger of a fanatical outburst on the part of his followers, as was shown after the feeding of the five
thousand. Besides, Herod himself had grown
jealous and uneasy and was likely to cause trouble.
So Jesus spends the hot summer away from Galilee,
chiefly in the mountain districts. He has a summer
school in theology. What a joy to have been one
of that little company. They appear in several
places and are not entirely alone even in the heathen
regions. But, on the whole, it is a summer of
freedom from disturbance and of intimate fellowship.
Jesus unburdens his heart to the men of his choice
as far as they will allow him.

2. *The Trip to Phœnicia.*—The work of Jesus
was limited mainly to the Jews for clear reasons.
They were the chosen people, the people of promise.
They must have the first chance. To work much
in Samaria or in Phœnicia would prejudice the Jews
generally against the gospel. Hence Jesus spent
most of his ministry in Jewish territory. Now he
is on heathen ground and will be for most of the
summer, but his work is chiefly with the disciples.

Jesus is the Saviour of the world as the Samaritans
saw and as he himself accented, but he was to begin
with the Jew. To the Jew first and then to the
Gentile. All this must be borne in mind and yet
Jesus did mingle with the Gentiles and was destined

by his gospel of grace and liberty to break down the
middle wall of partition between Jew and Gentile,
as he had already indicated in his teaching concerning eating with unwashed hands.   He even seems
to have entered a Gentile house (Mark 7 : 24)
though he would have no man know it.   However,
his seclusion seems due to a desire for quiet from
the crowds rather than to any sense of ceremonial
defilement such as Peter felt in the house of Cor-
nelius.

The reluctance of Jesus to heal the daughter of
the Syrophœnician woman is not hard to understand
in the light of what has just been said.   It was not
hardness of heart on the part of Christ.   It is to be
noticed that Jesus did not abruptly send her away
as the disciples suggested.   He heard her plea,
though he made it plain that his mission was first to
the lost sheep of the house of Israel.   He tested the
woman and brought out the greatness of her faith.
He did grant her request, a thing that the disciples
would not have done.   The disciple is often nar-
rower than his master.   The cleverness of this
woman is as striking as her faith.   "Even the little
dogs (κυνάρια) eat of the crumbs which fall from
their master's table."   She deserved a hearing for
that bright turn to the Master's protest.   Jesus did
not long tarry here, but went on from Tyre up

north to Sidon, though we have no further details of this journey. One would infer that the work done was less than in Galilee, though it is to be recalled that when Jesus preached the Sermon on the Mount there were people present from the seacoast of Tyre and Sidon. Hence Jesus was not an entire stranger to the Phœnicians and many more had heard of the wonderful Galilean Rabbi.

3. *In Decapolis.*—They kept to the mountains after leaving Sidon. Mark briefly sketches the journey as from Sidon through the borders of Decapolis to the seacoast of Galilee. This would mean probably a journey east from Sidon, then south and to the east of the Sea of Galilee into the high cliffs to the southeast. This is still heathen territory. The Decapolis was a league of Greek cities which were practically entirely Hellenized after Alexander's conquest. The teaching of Jesus in this region as well as in Phœnicia shows that he used Greek when necessary. The people here "were astonished beyond measure" at the healing of the deaf and dumb man, and they wondered as they saw the dumb speaking, the maimed whole, and the lame walking, and the blind seeing: and they glorified the God of Israel. As elsewhere, therefore, so here also the work of Jesus made a marvellous impression. In the modern sense of the term Jesu'

was here a foreign missionary. These Greeks glorified "The God of Israel." It was to the north of this section a little that Jesus had come when he healed the wild demoniac with a legion of demons. As a result of that excitement, though no Pharisees are here, Jesus charges them all not to tell about the healing of the deaf and dumb man. "But the more he charged them, so much the more a great deal they published it" (Mark 7 : 36).

There was here also a feeding of four thousand similar to that of the five thousand at Bethsaida Julias. Some critics cannot see how such a thing could have happened twice, although Mark and Matthew mention in detail both incidents and each records that Jesus referred to both incidents as separate. Other distinctions, like the name of the baskets on the two occasions, are preserved also. One can be too particular as well as too credulous. Nature works in great variety, but with marvellous similarity also. It is remarkable how in each great region where Jesus labored similar events take place, as in Judea, Galilee, Perea, and to a less extent in Samaria, Phœnicia, Decapolis, and the region of Cæsarea Philippi. People are very much alike after all. Christ delivers the same teachings in these regions with modifications here and there, and he works the same kind of cures. The people

are astonished everywhere. The slowness of the
disciples to obey the Master in the case of the four
thousand after their experience with the five thousand
is not to be wondered at too greatly. The dullness
and forgetfulness of the disciples concerning these
two incidents were pointedly condemned by Jesus.
Besides their slowness here is not an isolated instance,
but is a characteristic of their whole experience before the coming of the Holy Spirit. The surroundings in the case of the four thousand are quite different and the points of likeness are such as belong to
the nature of the case.

4. *A Brief Visit to Galilee.*—One day Jesus went
with the disciples over to the other side into Galilee.
We do not know exactly where the parts of Dalmanu-
tha or Magadan were, except that it was on the
western side, possibly down towards Tiberias. He
has been absent from Galilee for some time now.
How will he be received? Instantly, the ubiquitous
Pharisees came forth and began to question him,
as if they had missed him and were so glad to see
him back. The Sadducees are with the Pharisees,
a strange combination. The Herodians had already taken sides with the Pharisees against Jesus
and now the Sadducees do so. Christ had united
all three parties on one point at any rate, hostility
to himself. This is the first time that the Sad-

ducees are mentioned in the Gospels and the only one till the Passion Week. On the last day of Christ's ministry in the temple these three parties will appear together against Jesus. Here they have nothing new to say. They ask for a sign from heaven in proof of his claims as the Pharisees had done before.

Jesus "sighed deeply in his spirit." So this is his reception in Galilee! It is as hopeless as ever, in fact more so. Jesus answered them with reproach and denial. They could tell the weather, the face of the heaven, but not the signs of the times. They could not tell a sign from heaven if they saw one. He repeats this answer to the same demand made in Capernaum. He will give them the sign of Jonah. This enigmatic allusion perhaps only puzzled them. It was useless to explain. So Jesus abruptly left them and Galilee. He took boat with the disciples and turned up towards Bethsaida Julias on the northeastern shore.

On the way he pointedly warned the disciples against the leaven of the Pharisees, the Sadducees, and Herod. He had just been in the land of Herod and had been attacked by the Pharisees and the Sadducees. The disciples are hopelessly at sea with this simple simile and rather jejunely reply, "We have no bread!" (Mark 8 : 16). They did not have any kind of bread and so Jesus need not

caution them against the particular brand of the
Pharisees, Sadducees, and Herod! No wonder
Jesus was led to rebuke them sharply. He asked if
they had a mind, if they had eyes, if they had ears.
Their dullness seemed incomprehensible. Perhaps
every teacher has moments of sympathy with this
mood of Jesus here. Christ patiently explained
about the five thousand and the four thousand and
then said that by leaven he meant teaching. Did
they now understand? They saw dimly like the
poor blind man who at first saw men as trees walking.

5. *The Examination of the Twelve.*—It was time
for examination. They had now had a special summer course with Jesus in addition to all the rest. So
he took the disciples up to the slopes of Hermon
in the region of Cæsarea Philippi. He still kept
away from Galilee. Philip was a milder ruler and
a better man than Herod Antipas. He had tried
Galilee (Bethsaida, Chorazin, Capernaum, and all
the rest) and it had been found wanting. But after
all it mattered little what Galilee thought of him,
provided these men were clear and loyal. They had
been true that day in Capernaum, but a deeper
probing was necessary. They are here by themselves
and Jesus had been praying alone.

So on the way he took it up with them. He first
asked what men thought of him or said he was

He knew that well enough already, but it served as a
background for their own attitude.   It was a crucial
moment when Jesus abruptly asked: "But who say
ye that I am?" (Matt. 16 : 15).   They had taken
him as the Messiah at the start, it is true, but they
knew little about him then.   They had their own
preconceived ideas as to what the Messiah would be
like.   He had not come up to that.   The discovery
of that fact had sent the Galilean populace away in
disgust.   The twelve had been loyal.   He had told
them much more about himself.   What do they
think now after they know so much of the truth
about him?   Do they still think him to be the Messiah, the Son of God?   Or have they felt the force
of uncertain popular opinion which is now much
divided?   Few among the people now hold him to
be the Messiah, though many consider him John the
Baptist come to life or Elijah or Jeremiah or one of
the prophets.

It was Peter who found his tongue first and spoke
as he had done that day in the synagogue in Capernaum.   He rose to the dignity of the occasion.   Jesus
had said that Simon would be a Rock.   "Thou art
the Christ, the Son of the living God" (Matt. 16 : 16).
They are noble words and rightly expressed his conviction and that of the rest.   They did not indeed
fully understand all that these words signified, but

they could joyfully use them as their creed about Jesus. The heart of Jesus was made glad by these words and he made no effort to conceal the fact. Now Simon was worthy of his name. On this truth, trust in Jesus as the Son of God, rested the Kingdom of God, his glorious church. What Peter has done, all will do who come into the Kingdom. They will take Jesus as the Son of God and Saviour. In this clear confession Jesus sees the sure promise of victory. Satan had often tried to overturn him, but it is now clear that these men will be true and will carry on the work of the Kingdom. The gates of Hades will not be able to prevail against the Church or Kingdom of Christ. Peter and all the rest, all teachers of Christ, have the keys of the Kingdom, all who proclaim life to men on these terms. God will stand by the acceptance or rejection of Christ as His Son.

Not yet does Jesus wish them to tell others what is a great secret. It would set the land ablaze if the great truth came to be preached as yet. There is much more that they themselves need to know. They have made good progress on this point. Will they be true when they learn this "more"? When they learn of his death, what will they do? So a shadow comes over the hour of joy, but Christ does not doubt the final outcome. The present situation

nas vindicated what Christ said. Look at the Kingdom of God to-day in the world.

6. *The New Great Lesson.*—It seemed like a
mockery of all their hopes that now just as they
had made afresh the great confession, Jesus should
announce his death. There was no mistaking his
words. He had indeed heretofore used symbolic
language that pointed to his death, but it was all so
veiled that little impression was made. It is in fact
a distinct epoch in the career of Jesus, and Matthew
says that "from that time began Jesus to shew"
(Matt. 16 : 21) that he must be killed at Jerusalem.
Observe "must" and "at Jerusalem" and "at the
hands of the chief priests and scribes." So he expects the Sadducees and Pharisees to kill him after
all. All this was not only disconcerting to the disciples; it was absolutely depressing. It is true that
Jesus said also that he would rise on the third day,
but this ray of hope was always obscured by the
dreadful darkness of his death. That overshadowed
all else. The eclipse was coming and they were in
the penumbra. Jesus spoke of his death "openly"
and without parable.

Peter felt so strongly this chilling of their Messianic
hopes that he even took Jesus aside and dared rebuke
him for talking so. Of course Peter knew more of
what Jesus ought to do than Jesus himself! This

audacity was grounded in solicitude to be sure, but none the less it was inexcusable. Besides, he was grossly in the wrong. He did not understand the philosophy of the Messianic Kingdom. He did not know that self-sacrifice was the law of life, that one who tries to save his life shall lose it, that every man must take up his own cross if he means to follow Jesus. Already his cross is before the eye of Christ, as it was a familiar figure to all the Jews in Roman times.

All this goes to explain the sharpness of the rebuke that Jesus administered to Peter for his presumption. "Get thee behind me, Satan" (Matt. 16 : 23). It was a hard name, to call a disciple Satan, and especially Peter who had so recently been the spokesman in calling Jesus the Son of God. He is acting the part of Satan now as he was like a rock then. "Thou art a stumbling block to me." That was the point. Peter was tempting Jesus to do the very thing that the devil had urged. The most prominent of the disciples was actually persuading him not to die for the sins of men! It was a strange coalition, Peter and Satan! The devil had used Peter once and he will try again. He has discovered a way to handle the very foremost of the disciples. If he could only win him wholly! Peter was minding the things of men, not the things of God. Unconsciously he had taken the devil's point of view about the career of Jesus. It was a shock to Christ to have it come from Peter. It was a rude awakening to Peter, this agony of Jesus, but a necessary one. It was now clear that the disciples were far from being ready for the great catastrophe. Can they be made ready in time? How can they reconcile his Messiahship with his death? That was a theological knot difficult of solution.

7. *Heavenly Light on the Subject.*—From the human point of view Jesus was absolutely without sympathy in the deepest things of his life. The circle had once widened, but now it was very narrow, and almost a point. The apostles were indeed faithful to him, but they could not comprehend the spiritual nature of his mission nor the necessity and significance of his death. They were in poor plight to be left alone in a world that understood him still less. How could they pass through the dark hour of his death? One can little imagine the loneliness of Jesus at this time. The Father was his only sympathizer. About a week after Peter's rebuke Jesus went up into a mountain one night to pray. He took with him Peter, James, and John, the inner circle within the twelve. Jesus cherished no hard feeling toward Peter. After all, did the rest know any more? There is no indication that Jesus was

expecting what came, though, of course, that is possible. Certainly the three disciples were not. In fact, while Jesus was praying they went to sleep, or were on the point of sleeping at any rate. If the spirit was willing, the flesh was very weak as it was in the Garden of Gethsemane. The transfiguration of Jesus took place as he prayed. Was it the glory brought from heaven by Moses and Elijah? Or was it the restoration of Jesus to his pre-incarnate state as he talked with these heavenly visitors? The miracle consists not in the glory, but in the presence of Moses and Elijah. If genuine, as I believe, we have full proof of life beyond the grave, and of heavenly recognition.

There was something unusual in the death of both Moses and Elijah. God buried Moses and took Elijah up in a chariot of fire. But Moses stood for the law and Elijah for prophecy. Both law and prophecy have representatives to speak with Jesus who is the gospel of grace. They spoke of the decease of Jesus, of his exodus from earth. They at least understood, and Christ's heart was comforted at this dread hour. No doubt the Father graciously sent Moses and Elijah to console the spirit of Christ in this time of darkness. In the strength of this meat he could go on steadily to the cross. We do not know the words that were

said, but they were words of comfort beyond a
doubt.

It would seem that another object in view was to
help these three disciples to look at the death of
Christ from the standpoint of heaven rather than
from that of the world or Satan.   A glimpse of the
larger vision was offered them here, but they were
so heavy with sleep that Peter blundered again.   He
did indeed like the glory all about him, so much so
that he wished to stay there always.   Luke says
(9 : 33) that he did not know what he was saying
when he suggested three tabernacles, but though
dazed he was talking.   They were afraid when they
saw the cloud overshadow and envelop them and
heard the voice out of the cloud.   The voice not
only identified Jesus as the Son of God, but ex-
horted that the disciples hear him, hear him especially in the matter of his death.

But it was soon over, and with Jesus they went
down the mountain.   Christ broke the silence by
telling them not to speak of what they had seen and
heard till the Son of man should rise from the dead.
Then they might tell for the consolation of others.
Meanwhile it was to be for their own strength.   But
over again they missed the point and went to ques-
tioning among themselves as to what the rising from
the dead should mean.   They did notice now his

allusion to the resurrection. But if he referred to
the resurrection at the end of the world, that was a
long way off. So they relapsed into confusion again.
They did ask Christ about the coming of Elijah, but
not about the real problem in their heart.

At the bottom of the mountain they found the rest
of the disciples harried by the scribes because they
had failed to heal a demoniac boy. When Jesus succeeded they learned that their own failure was due
to lack of prayer.

8. *Back in Galilee and Fresh Teaching about His
Death.*—Jesus wishes no one to know that he is in
Galilee now (Mark 9 : 30). His real work in Galilee is over. He attempts again to explain about his
death and resurrection "Let these words sink into
your ears!" (Luke 9 : 44). They did get in, but
"They understood not." It seemed concealed from
them somehow and they were afraid to ask further,
though they were exceeding sorry. It was really
hopeless and the hour was drawing nigh. The
Galileans did find out that Jesus had returned, at
least the tax-collector did, for the demand was made
that he pay the half-shekel for the temple-tax.
Jesus paid the tax for himself and Peter, though in a
rather unusual way.

9. *Rivalry among the Twelve.*—Surely the cup of
Jesus was full enough without this. And yet, after

all the careful teaching about his death and resurrection they go on parcelling out the chief places in an earthly kingdom among themselves. They get into a quarrel on the great ecclesiastical question as to which of them is greatest in the kingdom of heaven! Ecclesiastical jealousy is rife, therefore, right among the bosom friends of Christ and in his very presence. When he asked them what they were disputing about, they would not say. They had already asked him who was the greatest in the Kingdom. They did not wish him to know of their envy. So Jesus called a little child. Was it Peter's child? This little child should teach them. They had missed it all again and did not know the law of service that the least was the greatest, the one who humbled himself most to serve.

This is a pathetic incident, but the saddest part of it is that the lesson was not learned then or now. Soon John, the beloved John, showed a spirit of narrow intolerance that caused a rebuke from Jesus. John had seen a man casting out demons in the name of Christ. He actually cast them out, too! What was his offence? He did "not follow us!" That was all. John expected to be promoted for extra zeal in orthodoxy! Here we have a needed lesson in tolerance about methods of work for Christ. How little John here understood the spirit of Jesus. But Christ was patient with the narrowness of John as he is to-day with ours. What poor earthen vessels we are after all, with our bickerings, jealousies and prejudices. The wonder is that Jesus can use any of us in his service. We preach the spirit of service for other people and practice too often self-aggrandizement and self-seeking. It was pitiable then and it is lamentable now.

Christ cares for his little ones, those who are weak and tender in the faith. It is easy to be heedless and reckless of consequences to those who love Jesus. Sometimes the millstone is hung around the neck of those who wrong the people of God. It is not God's will that one of those little ones perish.

The spirit of forgiveness of injury is in opposition to that of self-aggrandizement. Jesus does not mean that a brother shall injure as a matter of policy and then turn around and demand that we forgive him. That is rather a cold-blooded proceeding. But he does mean that genuine repentance shall be followed by forgiveness. And real forgiveness is "from your hearts." The eternal need of this spirit is accented in almost every church in the land.

There are some who are very officious in their service of Christ, not to say flippant. Jesus discourages such loud followers and reminds them of the

privations ahead of them. At this particular time
Jesus had not where to lay his head. He was an
outcast in the land of his people. On the other
hand, if one wishes to follow Christ, he will not turn
back after having put his hand to the plough. He
will not turn back even to stay with a father till he
die. This is what the expression "Bury my father"
means. That was a pious duty, but the father
might live many years and service for God was im-
perative.

10. *Light Advice from the Brothers of Jesus.*—
Was Jesus going to the feast of tabernacles? It was
near that time now, the last of September. It had
apparently been a year and a half since Christ had
been in Jerusalem. To go now offered little of hope.
The brothers of Jesus had noticed his long absence
from Jerusalem at the public festivals. They probably knew also about his long and recent absence from
Galilee. So they come and taunt him with being a
secret Messiah as if he were rather ashamed of it.
They tell him to go up to Jerusalem and to do his
work "openly." There are always plenty of people
who know how to manage our business better than
we do ourselves, especially if they dislike us a bit.
It is amazing how much wisdom is misapplied. It
looks sometimes as if all of us have the wrong task,
to judge by the advice so freely and generously

given. But Jesus asserts his independence. He
will go to Jerusalem when he pleases and conduct the
affairs of the Kingdom as seems good to him. He
went up privately and not publicly, as they had suggested, and at his own time.

11. *Facing Jerusalem.*—So he was going to Jerusalem again. It is a significant event in his career.
He has returned from his seclusion, but not to make
new campaigns in Galilee. He has higher ends
than that. He will go to Jerusalem and bring
matters to a focus there. When that is done, the
end will not be far off. Will he win Jerusalem?
He goes through Samaria again and excites the
hatred of the Samaritans because his face was set
towards Jerusalem. When he went north it was
all right.

Once more James and John show a spirit of bitter-
ness and lack of self-control as they wish to call down
fire on a Samaritan village. They did not know
what spirit they were of, and certainly they missed
utterly the spirit of Christ. Is it with a heavy heart
that Jesus goes on to the storm-centre of militant
and hardened Judaism? They will not have him
in Galilee and he had already been rejected in Jerusalem. Heretofore Christ had been on the defensive
as to his enemies in the Holy City and had kept
aloof from them not only in Jerusalem, but lately

in Galilee also.   But now the Master boldly appears in Jerusalem, not on the defensive entirely.   His appearance then is in the nature of an attack upon the enemy's country.   Will it succeed?   Suppose Jesus should win Jerusalem to his cause.   Is it worth trying?

CHAPTER VI

THE ATTACK UPON JERUSALEM

"O Jerusalem, Jerusalem, which killeth the
prophets and stoneth them that are sent unto
her" (Luke 13 : 34).

JESUS will now make a series of attacks upon Jerusalem itself. He had come here in the beginning;
he will finish his career here. He will not, indeed,
be able to stay in Jerusalem continuously, else the
end would come at once. But there is nowhere in
Palestine where Jesus can gain a permanent foothold so long as the city of Jerusalem is wholly in the
hands of his enemies. They are intrenched behind
ages of tradition and walls of prejudice and pride.
Somehow the idea had gotten out that Jesus might
come to the feast of the tabernacles this time, possibly
from his brothers, possibly from the Galilean multitudes. But in the opening days of the feast he is not
present. All at once Jesus is the chief topic of conversation. Will he come? Where is he? What
do you think of him anyhow? The Galilean multitudes are divided over him. They had once been
almost unanimously on his side, but now it is not so.

In the murmuring like that in the synagogue at Capernaum, some take up for him and say: "He is a good man"—this at any rate, whether he is the Messiah or not.   But others stoutly protest: "Nay, but he leads the multitude astray."   This controversy was largely in an undertone because all knew that the Jews of Jerusalem hated Jesus.   No one from Galilee wished to be mixed up in the affair. But one day in the midst of the discussion Jesus settled all speculation on this point by appearing in the temple and teaching.

1. *The Jerusalem Conspirators Outwitted at Home.* —There he is!   What will his enemies do?   This was their opportunity.

They fail to arrest Jesus at the feast.   The first effect of his teaching is the astonishment of the hostile Jews that he can talk so well since he did not attend their rabbinical seminary in Jerusalem.   He had attended God's school, if they but knew it.   But that alternative they would not admit.   Jesus cut matters short by boldly charging them with wishing to kill him.   They are hushed to silence, but the Galilean multitude protest that no one sought to kill him.   They little knew; but the people of Jerusalem understood all about it and a group of them comment on the fact when they see Jesus (John 7 : 25) and even poke fun at the rulers for not arrest-

ing Christ. Their theology as to the origin of the
Messiah is interesting and Christ took notice of it.
His enemies resented the ridicule of the people of
the city and actually sought to seize him then and
there. But Jesus bore a charmed life as yet. His
hour had not come. Some of the Galilean multitude become outspoken champions of Christ. At
this time the Pharisees and Sadducees (chief priests)
ordered some officers to arrest him. Jesus, meanwhile, in mystic language announces his independence of them, which his enemies fail to understand, thinking he will teach the Greeks (as he did
indeed!) The people become more excited over his
words, taking sides for and against, some even
ready to seize him. But the soldiers sent for that
purpose stood and heard his wondrous words and
came back sheepishly to the Sanhedrin without
Jesus. The Sanhedrin stormed at the officers and
sneered at them and at the ignorant rabble who followed Christ. The officers had fallen under the
spell of the speech of Jesus, a tribute to his character as well. It is to the credit of Nicodemus that,
when Jesus was there under fire by the Sanhedrin,
he dared to make a point of law in his favor. He
has more courage now than when he went to see
Jesus by night, but he received scorn for his courage.

The rulers are exasperated by Christ after the

feast. The multitudes had left for their distant
homes, but Jesus remained a while in the city and
continued to teach in the temple. His teaching consisted of short, crisp sayings that drew attention.
One of these stirred the Pharisees mightily. "I am
the light of the world" (John 8 : 12), he said. It is
an astonishing saying, if one is not prepared to go
to the full length of the deity of Christ, indeed otherwise an impossible saying. The Pharisees took it
up instantly. The dispute turned on the claim of
Jesus that God was his Father. That was its justification and that the Pharisees would not admit.
Jesus stung them again by saying that, if they did
not believe in him, they would die in their sins.
"Who art thou?" they demanded. If he would
only say a plain word that they could lay hold of!
But he points to the cross as the proof that he is
what he claims to be (John 8 : 28), a proof that to
them was only a stumbling block. Still some of
the Pharisees were impressed and said that they
believed on him. But Jesus had been suspicious
of the Jerusalem converts the first visit (John 2 : 24),
and proceeded to test these new believers. He
offered them the freedom of truth, which they resented; he offered to make them true children of
Abraham, but they were insulted; he showed that
they were not children of God in the full sense and

they proved it by trying to kill Jesus, a man who told them the truth. This sublime claim of existence before Abraham was to them unendurable.

The Pharisees are twitted by a blind man who had been healed by Jesus. He had been a well-known beggar and had a regular place to sit. The opening of his eyes by Jesus created a stir among the man's neighbors. They were not satisfied with his simple narrative. They took the man to the Pharisees who knew everything, but it was pitiful, the embarrassment of these pious wiseacres. It was done on the Sabbath and therefore God did not do it. But then it was done, and who else but God could do it? Some argued that Jesus was a sinner, else he would not have done it on the Sabbath; others that the man was never blind at all. They proceeded to settle the facts in the case by logic! The doctors differed and the man's parents were appealed to. They identified the man and proved his blindness. So the Pharisees were in a corner. Their logic and theology were bound to be correct, but how to explain this miserable fact without admitting the natural impression as to Jesus was a puzzle! They had appealed to the devil as the explanation of the expulsion of demons, but that fallacy had been exposed. The devil at any rate would be more likely to put eyes out rather than open

them. They took this new turn. We admit the
fact, but deny the conclusion. You just admit that
Jesus is a sinner and we, well, we will admit that
you can see! The man saw the humor of the situation. He was no theologian, but he could see a
point as plain as this. He opened my eyes and you
cannot tell whence he is! That is strange, when
you know everything! Besides, we all know God
does not hear sinners. But my eyes are open!
They turned on him in a rage. "Thou wast alto-
gether born in sins, and dost thou teach us?" He
had cut to the quick. They cast him out of the synagogue, but Jesus then led him into the Kingdom
of God and gave him spiritual sight also.

The enemies of Christ have their picture drawn
by Jesus. They did not sit for it voluntarily, but
provoked the characterization by asking Jesus
"Are we also blind?" (John 9 : 40). He told them
the allegory of the Good Shepherd who knows his
sheep and whose sheep know him. There are thieves
and robbers who want to get the sheep, but who will
run at the sight of a wolf like a hireling. But the
Good Shepherd will die for his sheep, and the one
flock has Gentile as well as Jewish sheep. It was a
vivid picture and some of them cried out: "He hath
a demon, and is mad." Yes, but others said, "Can
a demon open the eyes of the blind?"

2. *A Campaign in Judea.*—There had been an early Judean ministry which was only too successful. Now, when Jesus has to leave Jerusalem, he turns again to the country round about. As yet no permanent impression had been made here. Judas Iscariot had come from the town of Kerioth, and in Bethany Jesus had one home that he could almost call his own. He needed it, too, as a place where he could find rest and sympathy. Lazarus, Martha and Mary all loved Jesus though they had different ways of showing it, and Jesus greatly loved them.

This Judean ministry is recorded only by Luke who fills out largely the events of the last six months, his distinctive contribution to the life of Christ. Many of the events are similar to those in Galilee and many of the teachings are almost identical. All this is perfectly natural. There were Pharisees in Judea and hence the blasphemous accusation is repeated. Some of the Pharisees showed courtesies also to Jesus here as some did in Galilee. But the breakfast with the Pharisee did not turn out well. He put on airs because Christ did not bathe before the meal so that he and his lawyer guests were all sorely rebuked for insistence on the externals to the neglect of the moral and spiritual. The breakfast seems to have been broken up in disorder. One of the sharp lawyers who tried to entrap Jesus fell into the pit himself, but we forgive him since he was the occasion of Christ's telling the parable of the Good Samaritan which has so richly blessed the world.   It is not strange that Jesus should send out a band of preachers in Judea with similar instructions to those given the twelve.   Luke told also of the sending forth of the twelve.   Christ followed after them also and their success was to him a prophecy of the downfall of Satan.

Some of the sayings of Jesus during this period (Luke 12) are much like portions of the Sermon on the Mount.   One must never forget that he repeated his sayings often and as a teacher ought to have done so.   In the abstract it is possible that Luke has here recorded what Jesus said in Galilee, but it cannot be assumed that Christ would not repeat his teachings in different parts of the country, or even in the same region.

The eagerness of Jesus to meet his fate comes out (Luke 12 : 49 f.).   He longs to see the fire blaze, to receive his baptism of blood.   One cannot wonder at this when he recalls what the Master has already undergone and how hopeless the task seems.   So few understand what he has to say and fewer still seek to put it into practice.   This outburst is not impatience but it helps us to catch a glimpse of the volcano of emotion locked in the Saviour's heart.

3. *In Jerusalem Again.*—Without the blare of trumpets Christ comes again. It is winter (the feast of dedication), about our Christmas time, and he is walking in the corridors of the temple. The hostile Jews gather round him at once with a petulant question of impatience. They want to know who he is and what he has to say about himself. Evidently his last visit made a profound impression on them, and they are still talking about it. "If thou art the Christ, tell us plainly" (John 10 : 25). The question was a legitimate one, but they wished to make a bad use of his answer. They knew very well who he claimed to be, but they wished to charge him with blasphemy. But Jesus would not say the word Messiah for another reason, because it would inflame the populace beyond control. So he stood his ground and repeated his claim of oneness with the Father. They jumped at this and hurled the charge of blasphemy at him for making himself equal with God. He did do that, but it was not blasphemy, for he was equal with God. He would not argue that point, however, but he used an *argumentum ad hominem* by showing how in their law the rulers with God's authority are termed gods. It was a deft turn, but did not appease them. If they could not argue with him, they could kill him. But he was swiftly gone.

4. *Beyond Jordan Again.*—The stay of Jesus in Jerusalem had been brief and the collision was sharp and soon over. He did not stop in Judea, but went first to Bethany beyond Jordan where John the Baptist had identified him and where he had won his first disciples. What memories would come to Jesus as he thinks over the past. In a sense he is now a fugitive from Jerusalem. Had he made a mistake in joining issue so quickly and so persistently with the Jerusalem religious leaders? Could he have been more conciliatory and more effective? The devil had offered him compromise and power. He will go on as he began. There is one item that glorifies the preaching of John the Baptist. These people knew Jesus because of what John had said about him. That is a pertinent and a piercing test of modern preaching.

Luke alone gives us the story of this Perean ministry, save a few verses from John, but not much is preserved. We have to think over what we know about the work in Galilee and Judea and imagine similar scenes here. There was a man who had a theological point that troubled him. He wanted to know how many would be saved. Jesus told him that he had better try to get to heaven himself. One point that comes out is the anxiety of the Pharisees lest Jesus shall fall into the hands of Herod Antipas

in whose territory he now is.   Christ understands
"that fox" very well and asserts his independence
both of Herod and of the Pharisees.   It is difficult
to make out the frame of mind of these Pharisees,
whether they were really friendly to Jesus, whether
they were mere cat's-paws of Herod who wished
Jesus to move on, or whether they were trying to in-
veigle Jesus back to Jerusalem.   Christ saw all that
was involved and said that he would go to Jerusalem
to die at the right time.   Meanwhile his heart went
out in sorrow over Jerusalem.

A Pharisee in Perea also invites Christ to breakfast and three parables were spoken by Jesus, one
to the guests, one to the host, and one to a guest
who made a pious and platitudinous remark (Luke
14 : 15f).   There were great crowds here also and
Jesus put them to the test much as he did in Galilee
and probably with the same result.   The hard conditions of discipleship, like hating one's father, etc.,
are to be interpreted in this light.   If the issue is
made between father and Christ, one must not hesitate.

It was in Perea also that the scribes and Pharisees
sneered at Jesus for receiving sinners and eating
with them as he had done in Galilee.   In the formal
defense made by him for his conduct in seeking to
win the publicans rather than the Pharisees, he takes

them at their own estimate of themselves, not meaning
that it was correct. But his answer was complete.
They assumed that they were righteous. Well and
good, therefore; they did not need Christ, while the
publicans did. Hence Christ came after the lost
sheep, the lost coin, the lost son. They were like
the elder brother and were sulking because publicans and harlots were entering the Kingdom of
Heaven. When he spoke further the story of the
Unjust Steward, the Pharisees scoffed at him, for
they were lovers of money. But they ceased scoffing
when he told the parable of the Rich Man and
Lazarus, though they hated him all the more. We
may thank the Pharisees for one thing. They fur-
nished the occasion for the most marvellous parables
in all the world.

5. *The Sanhedrin in Desperation.*—The raising of
Lazarus was for the purpose of glorifying God and
Jesus the Son of God (John 11 : 4). It was pre-
meditated and so a deliberate expression of divine
power right in the teeth of the enemies of Jesus.
The miracle has been fiercely attacked in modern
times, but if Christ is divine, the argument for its
reality stands. The larger purpose of Jesus here
explains his apparent indifference to the request of
the sisters and then his seeming recklessness from
the point of view of the disciples and especially of

Thomas who had the courage of despair. When he comes it is Martha who hints that Jesus has power with God even now. It is to Martha that he uses the supreme language of deity; "I am the resurrection and the life." It is Martha also who makes a confession of faith in Jesus as noble as that of Peter (John 11 : 27). With Mary he exhibits great emotion in spite of himself, and even at the tomb he has difficulty in controlling his feelings. Martha recoils at the last moment, but Jesus is now calm and masterful. It was a majestic moment when at his command Lazarus stepped forth out of the tomb. The bearing of Jesus was never more dignified nor more serene than at this instant. He knew that Lazarus would come forth.

The Jews had come in great numbers from Jerusalem to console the sisters, for Lazarus was a man of wealth and position. Many of those that saw Lazarus come out of the tomb believed on Jesus. Others went and told the Pharisees what had occurred, as if in search of help. They were on the point of believing too. It was clear that something had to be done, and that at once, or all would be lost and for good.

It was indeed outrageous. Jesus had done this wonderful deed right at Jerusalem without their help or permission. A meeting of the Sanhedrin was called to deliberate over the situation. They each asked the other: "What do we?" The answer was easy, for they were doing nothing. They predicted the loss of their place and of the nation by the Romans, putting place before patriotism. Caiaphas remarked that they knew nothing at all, in which he was correct. He suggested that they make a sacrifice of Jesus for the sake of the country. There was a deeper sense in his words than he knew, but his sense of the proposal was a failure. They did make a sacrifice of Jesus, but the nation was destroyed by the Romans and they did lose their places. It is an easy and an old way out of a difficulty to propose to get rid of the other man. By the death of Jesus there have been gathered into one the children of God scattered all over the world, but that was God's plan, not Caiaphas's purpose. But now at last a formal decision has been reached by the Sanhedrin to put Christ to death as soon as possible. It was intolerable that Jesus should raise the dead right at their doors. Of course, he was a deceiver! No amount of power or proof could change that fact!

6. *In the Mountains of Ephraim.*—Back into the wilderness Jesus goes near the region where he had been tempted of the devil after his baptism. It was a dark hour from the human point of view. This then was the outcome of the Jerusalem campaign.

Galilee at least had not tried to kill him save **at** Nazareth. True, Jerusalem had several times before attempted his life, but in a sporadic way. Now he had to meet the formal decision of the Sanhedrin. If anything, now the Sadducees are more active than the Pharisees in their hatred. One cannot doubt that there in the mountains of Ephraim the devil brought to the mind of Jesus all the points that told against him. He could remind Jesus how it might have been if his advice had been followed. It was just as he had predicted.

It was not too late now to mend matters on the same terms. The devil had influence with the Sanhedrin and could easily call them off from their murderous purpose! But Jesus had fought this battle long ago. He would go to meet his hour. He had the disciples with him now in the wilderness, but how little they understood the tragedy that was going on before their very eyes.

7. *Going to Face the Issue.*—The hour is near at hand and Jesus leaves the hills of Ephraim. At first it looks as if he were going away from Jerusalem for he turns north through Samaria and into the edge of Galilee. But it is only to join one of the caravans from Galilee for the passover feast. His brothers had once suggested that he go down in public. Now he will do so. He will go to Jerusalem

as a King, the King Messiah. In the throng would
be some followers of Jesus and many who were more
or less friendly. The Pharisees who are along seem
to feel that something is in the air. They ask Jesus
when the Kingdom of God comes. He does not
answer that question, but the one that lay back of
it, the character of the Kingdom. Men will not see
it with their eyes nor point it out as here or there.
It is in the hearts of men, "within you" (Luke
17 : 20f.). The Pharisees make no reply, for the
answer of Jesus made the gulf between them still
wider. This was not the sort of a Kingdom that
they wished. To the disciples Jesus proceeded to
talk of his second coming. That subject looms
up before his mind now as his death draws so near.
The Son of Man will be fully revealed. Meanwhile
he gave an immortal picture of the Pharisee who
went up into the temple and gave the Lord a great
deal of pious information about himself and called
it prayer. The publican was "the sinner" and knew
it, but the Pharisee had to wait till the next world
to find out how big a sinner he was. The procession
goes on through Perea. Now the story is told by
all the Synoptics.

The Pharisees seek to catch Jesus on the question
of divorce. They were divided on it themselves,
one side favoring easy, the other, hard divorce. In

either case Jesus would hurt himself. ⸰ But they were amazed as he cut through their pettifogging scruples to the eternal principle of marriage and showed that Moses' bill of divorcement was due to the hardness of the hearts of the people and was a great advance for that time. The attitude of Jesus towards children comes out well here. Even the disciples regarded them as in the way. Christ has made the true place for the child in the world. No wonder they love him.

Jesus had to correct the ideas of the disciples about money. They actually supposed money proved that one was a favorite of heaven! The tendency to-day is to think that poverty is a proof of piety! One young man found out how much he loved money, more than he did Christ. Jesus makes another effort to teach his disciples about his death and uses the word "crucify" this time. His looks made the disciples amazed and afraid, but they understood them not. They were merely dazed for a moment and right away James and John with their mother come up and beg the two chief places for themselves in the Kingdom! What Kingdom? What places? It was pitiful, and at such a time! Jesus offered them the martyr's cup, the baptism of death, which they lightly accepted. How little they knew the philosophy of the Kingdom. Even the son of Man had

come to give his life a ransom for many (Luke
18 : 45). The ten, of course, were indignant, not
that they were themselves innocent of the same
spirit.

8. *The Challenge to Jerusalem.*—Jesus is at Jeri-
cho and all is astir. Blind Bartimeus and Zac-
cheus are but incidents by the way. He was nigh
to Jerusalem and the people supposed that the
Kingdom of God was immediately to appear (Luke
19 : 11). They felt it in the air. Their sort of a
Kingdom was now to appear. The real Kingdom
had already come and was continually coming.

Jesus told the parable of the Pounds to discourage
their false expectations, and yet he had decided to
gratify the people to a certain extent. He went on
up toward Jerusalem to Bethany. Here with the
Bethany family he can spend the Sabbath in rest
and quiet. Great events are ahead of him and he
needs the respite. In Jerusalem itself all was on
the *qui vive* as to whether Jesus would come to the
feast or not now that the Sanhedrin had decided to
kill him. They had made public request for his arrest, perhaps by placard in the temple courts. Out
at Bethany many came not only to see Jesus, but
Lazarus also. The feeling was tense at both places,
in Jerusalem antagonism, in Bethany sympathy. In
Bethany with his dear friends he had a sweet haven

and the sun shone on Olivet, but the clouds hung low over Jerusalem.

Jesus knew that the people could not understand his claim to be Messiah without plainer language than he had used. He will now employ the language of action, well knowing that his death was the reward for his boldness. His enemies had long wished him to say in plain terms that he is the Messiah. That wish will now be gratified. The picture of Jesus that Sunday morning on the colt of an ass, as Zechariah had said the King Messiah would ride, was not one to strike terror to the heart. He was King of Peace, and yet as the multitude from the city joined the multitude from the village, and all turned down the slope of Olivet toward Jerusalem the Pharisees who saw it thought that all was over. This popular demonstration meant to them that Jesus had won. They would not dare lay hands on him while he had so many friends. So they turned and blamed each other for this outcome. "Behold, how ye prevail nothing: lo, the world is gone after him" (John 12 : 19). Others of the Pharisees sought to shame Jesus into rebuking his disciples for the uproar (Luke 19 : 39).

But they are hailing Jesus as the Son of David. The Kingdom of God has come at last. Hosannah. Peace in heaven and glory in the highest. If these had stopped now, the very stones would have cried out. The clamor grew worse, for in the temple courts the very boys took up the strains from the crowd, to the chagrin of the chief priests and scribes who even sought to get Jesus to stop that. With a look around upon all this scene Christ went back to Bethany with the disciples. What did they think of the Master now? For the moment he was Master indeed, the hero of the hour and in Jerusalem at that.

9. *A Foretaste of the Struggle.*—Jesus had crossed the Rubicon and now the issue was to be fought out. The exasperation of his enemies increased as he came to the temple next day to teach. He cleansed the temple again as he had done at the beginning and this maddened the rulers still more. The popularity of Jesus was unendurable. They came early to get standing room about the great Teacher and hung on his words listening. He was the centre of all eyes. The rulers had found out where he was very well, but what to do with him was the problem, for they feared this multitude.

Some Greeks at the feast heard of him and courteously asked of Philip to be presented to him. But Philip felt embarrassed by the request and consulted Andrew the man of counsel. But even Andrew was not able to untie this knot. They bring the problem, but not the Greeks, to Jesus for his decision. The middle wall of partition between Jew and Greek Jesus had come to break down, but there was only one way to do it. Greeks will come to him indeed, as will all classes of men, when he is lifted up. The law of life is death, as Christ explains by the grain of wheat. Jesus in profound words sets forth the principle of his atoning death, the voluntary giving of his life for men. So vivid does all this become to him, as he contemplates his hour, that in agony as in Gethsemane he cries out to the Father to save him from this hour (John 12:27), but with instant submission. "Father, glorify Thy name." This, then, is Christ's idea of his death: it is a glorification of the Father's name. Once more, the third time, the Father speaks in audible voice words of approval. The Father thus understands this view of his death. No one else at that hour understood either him or the Father. The darkness of the eclipse is coming on.

10. *The Victorious Debate.*—The rulers felt keenly their disadvantage now before the people. There was the raising of Lazarus, the triumphal entry, the cleansing of the temple, the marvellous teaching. The spell must be broken somehow. He must be exposed and made ridiculous, if nothing more. Tuesday morning, as Jesus walked and taught in the

corridors of the temple with admiring crowds of listeners, he suddenly found himself confronted by a company of the rulers who challenged his authority. But all at once they are themselves on the defensive as Jesus by a pertinent question asked their opinion of John's baptism. John had introduced, baptized, and identified Jesus as the Messiah. If John's baptism were of God, that was the answer to their question, for he was the Messiah. But the question of Jesus put them in a hopeless quandary, and they timidly begged to be excused, and so they are laughed at, not Jesus. Christ pressed his advantage by then telling parables which the rulers saw were against them, but which they were helpless to turn. They stepped back, cowed, saddened, but no wiser. The Pharisees and Herodians rallied and came to the rescue by sending some of their brightest students to ask a question about tribute to Cæsar. The people, of course, were opposed to the Roman taxes and hated the publicans who collected them. But to oppose the taxes publicly was treason against Cæsar. It was with a deal of pious palaver that these youngsters gave him what they thought was a hopeless dilemma. But at the reply of Jesus they looked simple, held their peace, and stepped back, wondering greatly at finding one wiser than they were. The Sadducees enjoyed the defeat of the

Pharisees and Herodians and tried now their hand with a stock story about the resurrection which the Pharisees had never been able to meet. But Jesus showed by the word of God to Moses that they were in error, not knowing the Scriptures. They, too, were silent, but the Pharisees (scribes) could not keep still. "Master thou hast well said" (Luke 20 : 39).

At this the Pharisees gathered in a jubilant group and one of the lawyers among them volunteered his services to his embarrassed friends. He tempted Jesus by a question in his own specialty, the law. He could only acquiesce in the reply of Jesus and retire. Our Lord now turned on the assembled Pharisees and asked them a question about the person of the Messiah, the very thing that they had so often asked him. How could he be the Lord of David and the Son of David at the same time? The problem really was that of the humanity and the divinity of the Messiah. He had carried the war into Africa and put them all to rout. No one dared ask him another word. "The common people heard him gladly."

They were still cowering before Jesus, and for once he let loose the vials of his wrath upon his relentless foes. He called attention to the high position of these teachers and how they had degraded

their office. They hid the truth, they made prose-
lytes worse than they were before, they were mere
hair-splitters, they put wrong emphasis on truths,
they were ceremonialists without the spirit, they
were professional religionists, boasters of heredity,
in a word hypocrites, serpents, offspring of vipers,
with the judgment of hell upon them. It was ter-
rific; before this hailstorm and lightning his enemies
shrunk away and the crowd dispersed. The heart of
Jesus bursts out in lament over Jerusalem soon to be
desolate, while the disciples gathered in silence apart.
Jesus sat down in exhaustion and watched the people
cast their gifts into the treasury, especially one poor
widow whose piety doubtless cheered him. All was
quiet now after the storm. He went out of the
temple, his Father's house, for good and all. His
enemies were like maddened hornets.

11. *The Prophecy of Doom.*—As they went out
Jesus pointed to the fine temple buildings and prophesied the destruction of them all. It sounded, as it
was, like an echo of his recent denunciation of his
enemies. The desolation of Jerusalem would be
due to their treatment of him. The debate had
closed with Christ as complete victor. But Jesus
knew that people are seldom convinced against their
will by debate. They would answer him in some
other way. Behind the death of Christ lies the de-

struction of Jerusalem. Further in the background
still lies the end of the world. As Jesus sat on Olivet
and looked down at the city that he had longed to
save, all these catastrophes pressed upon him and
blend into one common picture. Language after
all is pictographical. It is hardly possible to separate all the details of each part of this composite
picture of doom. And Jesus expressly disclaimed
knowledge of the time of the end of the world,
though he expected the destruction of the city to
come in that generation, as indeed it did. Escha-
tology is not a lucid subject at best and on this occasion the double theme makes it extremely difficult
for us. But the Kingdom of God will be taken from
the Jews and given to the Gentiles. The doom of
the city will be in one sense a coming of Jesus again
in judgment and will symbolize the final coming.
The main practical lesson then and now for us is to
be ready. The very uncertainty demands diligence,
not carelessness. It is easy to say that Jesus was
mistaken because he has not yet come, but one who
believes in Jesus as Lord will prefer to wait and trust
and be ready. They left the summit of Olivet and
went down to Bethany that night. What a day it
had been! What thoughts were in the hearts of
Jesus and the disciples!

CHAPTER VII

THE ANSWER OF JERUSALEM

"Crucify, crucify him" (Luke 23 : 31).

But it was not yet to rest that Jesus went to Bethany.
His friends there had a social service to render him.

1. *An Appreciative Group in Bethany.*—They did
not meet at the house of Mary and Martha but with
Simon, who had been a leper (not Simon the Pharisee), and who wished to show his love and gratitude
to Jesus. Christ had told his disciples that after
two days he would be crucified, thus for the first
time setting a date for the event. Their hearts, at
least, would be heavier than usual during the feast.
John mentions this feast out of place in connection
with his last account of Bethany, but we follow
the Synoptic order.

Lazarus was there back from the grave, and Jesus
was there soon to die. The occasion thus brought
forth mingled emotions. It was Mary of Bethany,
not Mary Magdalene, whose spiritual devotions found
fit expression in the ointment with which she anointed
his head and his feet. She wiped his feet with her
hair. She had caught the truth about his death

and thus delicately expressed her love for the Master. It would seem that even those who would not thus have shown their feelings toward Christ could at least have been willing for Mary to do so. But every one of the disciples followed the lead of Judas in his blunt and brutal protest against Mary's wasteful extravagance. She found a champion, however, in Jesus, who understood her motives and approved her deed, interpreting it for the dull disciples. But it was a distinct rebuke to Judas and, as it proved, the last straw that was needed to break the back of his impatience.

2. *The Sanhedrin Receive Unexpected Help.*—At the very hour of this feast when the rulers had met in Jerusalem to talk over the situation, they were stung beyond endurance by the triumph and defiance of Jesus that morning in the temple, and all the more so that now they felt so helpless. They had before the passover made public proclamation of their purpose to arrest Jesus, but now they timidly feared his power with the people. It is evident that they must take Jesus by stealth, and after the passover is over and the crowds have gone. This is the part of wisdom as all agree. They are still determined to kill him to save the state and themselves. But all at once Judas, one of the twelve disciples, steps into the room. At first, perhaps, the conspirators are

stunned and fear some new attack from Christ,
but Judas relieves their fears by blurting out:
"What are ye willing to give me and I will de-
liver him unto you?" (Matt. 26 : 15). What else
he said to convince them of his sincerity we do not
know.

He may have said that he was tired of the whole
business, that there was nothing in it for him, and
he would like to see the bubble burst as soon as possible. In his heart he was disappointed that Jesus
was going to die and not be the kind of a Messiah
that he expected; perhaps envy had arisen toward
Peter, John and James. Jesus had proven to be an
idle dreamer and had thrown away his opportunity.
At the feast, this very night, he had given him a public insult while the money bag was empty. He knew
the haunts and habits of Christ at night, his place
of prayer, for instance, and so could easily catch him
if they would furnish the soldiers. They must not
wait till after the passover feast. It could be done
right away. The Sanhedrin were convinced. It
seemed providential to these pious murderers, this
opportune convert, and one right from the very circle
of Jesus' friends. Who could have believed such
good fortune possible? They were glad, which was
more than they had been for a long time. The price
agreed on was the price of a slave, thirty pieces of

silver, and perhaps was meant in that sense. It now remained for Judas to fulfill his contract. Whatever the motives that prompted Judas were, clearly he was now wholly in the power of the devil. It is amazing how common turncoats are, men who are easily rebuffed and wish to show their spite. The act of Judas was secret, but it did not escape the knowledge of Christ. Did Judas suspect next day that Jesus knew? The day was spent in rest at Bethany, for it was useless now to go again to Jerusalem to teach anyone. The die had been cast and Jesus would take the consequences.

3. *Jesus' Concern for the Disciples.*—How will they stand the awful catastrophe before them? Christ will make one more effort to prepare them for his arrest, condemnation and death. Peter and John are sent to make ready the passover, and at the evening hour at the time of the regular passover meal the disciples assemble in Jerusalem with Jesus in the supper-room, perhaps in the house of Mary, the mother of John Mark. The heart of Jesus is stirred with emotion before he suffers (Luke 22 : 15 f). Judas had put on a bold front and come in, but besides his presence the contention of the twelve for the chief place grated on the spirit of Christ (Luke 22 : 24 f), and finally led to his rebuking them by an object lesson of humility (John 13 : 15). It

was a poor start for this last passover to begin in such a fashion.

But this, bad as it was, was a small matter compared with what Christ had to disclose to them. One of them was going to betray him to the Sanhedrin. The thing seemed incredible, but Jesus had said it. With startled faces they looked at each other and then at Jesus, one after the other asking, "Is it I, Lord?" Of course Judas had to ask also. Peter motioned to John to ask Jesus who it was, but the disciples did not seem to understand the sign given by Christ nor to have heard what he said to Judas when he went out. But he was gone and it was night.

Jesus drew closer to the eleven and his heart went out to them. He urged that they love one another, those who had just contended for the chief places. Satan was after them all, had Judas for good, and was hard after Peter.

But Jesus had prayed especially for Peter so that he would stand the sifting. Peter really thought the anxiety of Christ needless in his case. He had forgotten how he had once played the part of Satan. So all felt, but Peter was vehement in his assertion of readiness to die for Jesus, if necessary. If they only knew! They will need to struggle now and to fight, though not with literal swords as they understood Christ, but Jesus cannot explain further, for they would not understand. Probably the Lord's Supper was instituted by Christ after Judas left, if we follow the order of Mark and Matthew and not Luke. There was a hush in the upper chamber as Jesus talked on of his death, symbolized by this ordinance. He really meant to die. That was perfectly plain. It is John who has preserved for us this unbosoming of the heart of Christ. He told them all that they could bear and more than they then understood about the Father, the Son, the Holy Spirit, and the future of Christianity. But the insistent note in it all was their need of faith in Jesus after his death. They must believe in him as they believed in God, for he was one with the Father whom he had manifested to them in himself. They can pray to him also and he will hear. He will send the Holy Spirit besides to take his place as comforter and guide to truth and life. They must, in a word, abide in him and love one another, for the world will hate and persecute them. But after all it was best for them that he go away, best for their own development, best for the progress of the Kingdom of God. The new Teacher will explain Jesus himself to them and then they will know what he is now trying to make clear. Besides he will come back to them. They will see him in a little while when he returns

from the grave.   They will have his presence through
the Holy Spirit even after his ascension.   Moreover,
he will at death take each one of them to the Father.
He will come again at the end of the world.   He
himself came from the Father and is going back to
the Father.

Thomas, Philip, Judas (not Iscariot), at first
asked questions, as he talked, but soon all was
silent attention.   Now at last they seem to apprehend the meaning of Jesus.   They know and believe, they say.   If they only did!   Christ had said
all to them that was worth while.   But he could talk
to the Father about them.   Either while still in
the upper room or possibly in the moonlight on the
street outside, Jesus stopped and prayed a wonderful
prayer about himself, these eleven men and the other
disciples through all the ages.   As for himself he
longed to go back to the Father, to the glory, to the
fellowship.   As for the eleven apostles, he had great
solicitude.   He had done his best with them while
with them, but now he is to leave them in the world
without him.   Will they leaven the world or will the
world master them?   Satan will seek to win them.
He prays that the Father will keep them now from
the evil one.   If only all the disciples in all the ages
can keep down bickerings, personal rivalries, jealousies, rancors, divisions on unimportant matters,

the world will soon know that Jesus is the Saviour of men and the Son of God. It is not organic unity that Christ has in mind. It is something far deeper, unity of Spirit and freedom from strife such as the disciples had shown this very night.

4. *The Struggle of Jesus with Himself.*—The Master had held up boldly while exhorting and consoling the disciples, but in reality he was in the depths himself. Every true preacher knows what it is to comfort other hearts while his own is breaking. But the reaction had to come after the strain of so much emotional talk. There were a few brief hours before the crisis came, and these Jesus would spend in prayer. He had the habit of going to the Garden of Gethsemane for prayer at night and this custom Judas knew and took advantage of it. In his greatest agony Jesus naturally sought this spot. Besides many obvious advantages, it was a comfort to him to be in the place where he had often communed with the Father. The very surroundings would help him in his hour of depression which he felt coming on. He never needed the support of prayer so much, not even in the dreadful temptations in the beginning of his ministry.

Christ knew that Judas would come here and so he divided the disciples, leaving eight near the gate and taking Peter, James and John further in to watch while he prayed.   Instantly Jesus "began to be greatly amazed" (Mark 14 : 33).   He had never felt that way before.   He turned to the three and said: "Pray that ye enter not into temptation" (Luke 22 : 40).   The temptation of all temptations was now upon him, to recoil from the cup which he had offered to drink.   He did not know it would be so bitter, and he had to take the very dregs of the cup.   He was free from sin, and now for sin to smite him was hard.   On his face on the ground he prayed, "O My Father," "Abba, Father" in the Aramaic of his childhood.   How could he endure to be looked upon as sin?   He cried out against the cup, but instantly he acquiesced in the Father's will, "as Thou wilt."   That was victory, to submit to the Father.   An angel from heaven strengthened him, and that was the Father's answer to his prayer. But the agony increased till his sweat became, as it were, great drops of blood (probable text of Luke). But in it all Jesus had won and now was calmer. He turns to the disciples and finds them asleep! They were only a stone's throw away, but they had gone to sleep as the Son of God battled with himself for human redemption.   It did seem hard if they could not watch at such a time for one hour.   They had no excuse to offer, save weariness, but they slept again through the two succeeding struggles of Christ.

How little they understood what it was all about.
How little sympathy they gave Jesus in his hour of
great need. But Christ had won the last great
battle with himself. He could go to Calvary now.
He would drink the cup. It matters little now
whether they sleep or not.

5. *Jesus Gives Himself up to His Foes.*—It should
never be overlooked that Christ made a voluntary
surrender of himself to his enemies. Vain the
Roman soldiers with all their weapons and torches,
vain all the treachery of Judas, vain the persistent
hatred of the Sanhedrin, if Jesus had not been
willing to die. He could call legions of angels to his
help. He did indeed smite the soldiers to the earth
with a word as he stepped forth to meet them.
Jesus rallied them for their timidity in coming there
by night instead of arresting him openly in the temple.

But Judas did not lose his nerve. He had taken
advantage of his knowledge of the devotional habits
of Jesus in order to betray him. His infamy was
to sink still lower when he gave the kiss as a sign to
the soldiers. Christ was shocked at this depravity.
Peter's blood was stirred at the baseness and he
wanted to fight. He did indeed try to kill Malchus, a
servant of the High Priest, and cut off his right ear
as he dodged his head. But Jesus would not allow
that much use of the sword for himself. He healed

the ear and insisted that the Scriptures must be ful-
filled. He must drink the cup. It was the hour
and the power of darkness (Luke 22 : 53). Christ's
hour and the power of light will come later. The
disciples were paralyzed with fear when Jesus refused to use his power to protect himself and for-
bade their doing anything. The spectacle of Christ
in bonds was too much for them. He had always
defeated his enemies before but now he would not
do anything. It was clearly time for them to take
care of themselves. Even Peter fled too, after all
his talk of courage. A young man, possibly Mark,
came near getting into trouble for following Jesus
after the arrest. He had to flee naked. Surely
blackness of night had now come. To Judas it
was all easier than he had thought.

6. *Jesus Faces His Accusers.*—Peter and John
followed him to the palace of the High Priest. John
went on inside, but Peter remained in the outer
court. Now Jesus is in the toils of his enemies.
At last they have him in their clutches after years
of effort. How they chuckled with satisfaction.
They will now show him who understands the law
and whose theology is right. They will answer all
his arguments by death. The logic of persecution
limps badly. The trouble is that the truth cannot be
killed though you kill the man who teaches it. The

vitality of truth is marvellous. But the persecutor never learns anything and unhesitatingly flings himself against eternal truth and the eternal God. There are two trials, the Jewish and the Roman, though, as a matter of fact, only the Roman was pertinent, for the Sanhedrin had already decided on his death, and did not have the power of death. Still it would look strange for them to demand his death without a trial and so they would go through the form of it. But nearly every form of law and every principle of justice is disregarded to get a conviction.

The Jewish trial has three stages in it, though the appearance before Annas is merely a preliminary examination by the ex-high priest probably, while the Sanhedrin is assembling. He asks Jesus about his disciples and his teaching with a fling at both. Christ with dignity appealed to the publicity and success of his work. His protest led a bystander to strike Jesus, who did not turn the other cheek, but made a calm, yet firm denial of the justice of that blow. Soon the Sanhedrin meets, possibly in the same palace, a full meeting, with the probable exception of Joseph and Nicodemus. Caiaphas presides and acts as chief prosecutor as well. It was illegal to try such a case at night, anyhow. The witnesses were hired and told nothing after all. The farce was at an end when two witnesses brought up what Jesus had said about the destruction of Jerusalem three years before, misconstrued it, and disagreed in the misconstruction. But the high priest had to pretend that something had been made out, and in a great rage demanded that Jesus defend himself. There was nothing to defend himself against, and, if there had been, he did not have to incriminate himself. It was only when the high priest put Christ on oath as to whether he was the Messiah or not that Jesus spoke. This, after all, was what was the matter. To refuse to answer now would have been proper legally, but would have been understood as a denial of his Messiahship. Then Jesus spoke with clearness, "I am." Moreover, the day will come when this Sanhedrin will stand before him who will sit at the right hand of power. This transcendent claim made it easier for them to have a show of right in voting that he was guilty of blasphemy. After dawn a ratification meeting was held, but no ratification can ever make a wrong right.

Somewhere in the midst of the Jewish trial the denials of Jesus by Peter took place. It is a sorrowful story and humiliating in the extreme. Peter had been specially honored and warned by Jesus, and had been loudest in his protestations of fidelity. He sought to hide in the crowd of servants by the fire in the open court, but the fire had light as well as heat. His exposure then led him to go to the door by the street, but even here he was recognized. He did conceal himself for an hour, but finally a kinsman of the high priest's servant, Malchus, whose ear he had cut off, said: "Did not I see thee in the garden with Him?" (John 18 : 26). That was enough, and Peter lost all control of himself, swore, and cursed like an adept in the business to prove his ignorance of Jesus. He caught the eye of Jesus through the open door, and the look broke his heart. He went out and wept bitterly, and appeared no more until after the resurrection. The Gospels vary in many details, but somehow thus these things seem to have occurred.

Before Pilate the accusers come with quite different charges. They now make political, not religious accusations. The first charge of perverting the nation was mere fiction. The second one of forbidding to give tribute to Cæsar was a downright falsehood, the very thing that they had tried to get Jesus to say. The third charge of claiming to be a king was true, but not a king in the sense that Cæsar was, as they well knew. In fact the chief complaint the Jews had against Christ's claiming to be the Messiah was just this, that he would not be a temporal king. The triumphal entry gave

enough color to the charge for them to use it. When
Pilate learns that he is king of truth, he sees that this
does not at all infringe on the province of Cæsar.
He even endeavors to persuade the Jews to be willing for Jesus to be set free, announcing his own decision that he is innocent. Surely this is a strange
attitude for a judge to assume. Pilate catches at
the mention of Galilee to send him to Herod Antipas,
who quickly sends him back. He was nothing but
a puzzle to him. He seeks to win favor for Jesus
by putting him against Barabbas in the choice of
the people as a released prisoner. But the chief
priests stir up the people to ask for Barabbas. Pilate
tries to make a joke out of the thing and brings out
Christ with a crown of thorns on his head. In disgust he surrenders, repeating the innocence of
Jesus, not his guilt. In superstitious dread he once
more recoils from the deed and the people shout
Cæsar at him. They will tell Cæsar that Pilate par-
doned a man who claimed to be a rival king. It
was their strong appeal, and Pilate withered before
it. Vainly did he remind the Jews that they had
done it, not he. He could wash his hands, but not
his soul. In truth, Sanhedrin, mob, Pilate, Judas,
all had their share in the crime of the ages. There
was guilt enough for all. The cry of the people to
crucify Jesus was a nightmare to Pilate and is a stain

upon the Sanhedrin, Sadducees, Pharisees, all, that
has never been erased.

7. *Jesus Dies a Shameful Death.*—It is a dreadful
story, a harrowing narrative, the tragedy of the universe. Jesus came to redeem Israel and Israel
crucified him. He came to his own, and his own received him not, preferred a highway robber to him,
took his blood on their heads with spiteful glee.

Jesus began the journey to the cross, carrying his
own cross, but Simon of Cyrene was shortly impressed to carry it after him, probably because of the
fatigue of Christ, exhausted by the fearful night.
The women of Jerusalem who bewailed his fate
little knew what would befall their fair city because
of this deed. Jesus reminds them of the fate of the
dry tree when once the flames light it up. In a sense
Christ took the place literally of Barabbas, who
would have been crucified between these two robbers as the ringleader of them. Upon the hill
shaped like a skull, overlooking the city, they nailed
Jesus to the cross. He would not take the wine
mingled with gall or myrrh, which some sympathetic
person offered him to relieve his sufferings. He
would go into the shadow with unclouded brain. He
would taste the whole cup.

The first three hours on the cross, from 9 A. M.
to 12 noon, were hours of torture and scorn. But

Jesus showed the sublimity of his spirit by praying for forgiveness for his murderers, who did not know in their blind rage what they were doing. He practised now what he had preached. But while he prayed, the soldiers gambled for his robe at the foot of the cross. Pilate had a spasm of stubbornness after his weak surrender on the main point. He stoutly refused to alter the accusation written on the cross. It was indeed the charge on which Jesus had been sentenced by him, but it stung the Sanhedrin. He would show them that he could not be run over all the time. The heart of Jesus went out to his mother who stood by the cross. The sword had indeed pierced her soul now. The brothers and sisters of Jesus did not believe in him yet and so John, the beloved disciple, is the only one who can console Mary in this unutterable hour. He led her away from the dreadful scene to his home in Jerusalem.

One of the bitterest drops in the cup was the mockery of the crowds as they swept by in lofty scorn. Jesus was now a fallen idol and they gleefully hurled into his teeth his great claims as Saviour, Son of God, the Christ, King of Israel, his power to build the temple in three days. Why not step down from the cross that we may see and believe? That will convert us all! So the crowds, the members of the

Sanhedrin, who lost control of themselves in their hour of triumph, so the soldiers with loud rudeness, so even the robbers on the cross by his side. Even the robbers looked down on this scapegoat between them, till one of them came to his senses and turned in rebuke to the other. The revulsion was so great in him that he swung over to faith in Jesus. That was trust, indeed, to believe that Jesus had a kingdom in such an hour as this. He trusted that a better day would come for Christ, and Jesus honored his faith then and there, and opened the portals of Paradise. Even on the cross Jesus saved a soul, aye, on the cross he saved all who are saved.

At noon came the black darkness, as if nature could not longer behold the scene. The veil of night is drawn over these three slow hours when silence reigned. The mocking ceased and a strange awe fell upon all. It was not an eclipse of the sun, for it was the time of the full moon. The stillness was at last broken by a cry of desolation from Jesus. He felt that somehow in all the dreariness of these hours the Father had withdrawn his presence. He was made to be sin, who knew no sin, and he was left to feel the sting of death for sin. We may not penetrate the mystery further, but someone has well said that the answer to this cry was John 3 : 16. It was God's love for the world that had made possible

this hour of unutterable gloom. Jesus retained his
consciousness of what he was doing. He took a sip
of vinegar and cried, "It is finished" (John 19 : 30).
He saw victory where the devil and the Sanhedrin saw
only defeat. He died with a cry of resignation on
his lips, and gave up his spirit to the Father.

And Jesus was dead. His head was bowed and
the light was gone out of his eye. The great artists
of all ages have sought to put on canvas this sublime
and awful tragedy. The temple had the veil rent
from top to bottom by the earthquake which came
when Jesus died. The graves of many saints were
opened, who themselves came forth after his resurrection, so Matthew records (Matt. 27 : 53). The
Roman centurion in charge of the crucifixion was
greatly impressed by the darkness, the earthquake,
and the bearing of Jesus. He realized that a dreadful mistake had been made and a good man put to
death. The people were smitten with dread and
fled to the city. The faithful women stood alone
and watched it all.

When the soldiers came to finish the work that the
bodies might not remain over the Sabbath, they
found Jesus already dead. John had come back to
the cross and saw a soldier pierce the side of Jesus
when blood and water came, proving thus two things:
One that he was a real man, and no mere phantom

because of the blood, the other that he had died rather suddenly because some blood still remained in him, probably from a broken heart, according to the suggestion of Stroud. The blood, so Dr. Stroud argues, would not otherwise be found in the body after death. But John, whatever the explanation, insists that his witness to the fact is true (19 : 35). The courage of Joseph and Nicodemus at this dark hour is not strange after all, just as timid women will often be bold as lions in a great crisis. They took this stand for Jesus after his star had sunk out of sight. Let it be put to the credit of those two men of high position that, though they waited long, they did take their stand openly for Christ when it cost most to do so, when in fact many of the leading disciples were in hiding. But the women were faithful. They watched the place, the new tomb of Joseph in the garden, where Jesus was laid, watched till the Sabbath drew on (dawned), and then rested with heavy hearts that night. It was a restless Sabbath that the rulers spent, for, though Jesus was dead, he had spoken of rising from the dead. They did not believe any such nonsense themselves, but the case of Lazarus made them uneasy. They feared Jesus, though dead, as Herod Antipas did John the Baptist. They gave it out to Pilate that they were afraid of the disciples of Jesus. At

any rate, they had their way and a guard was placed
by the sepulchre sealed with the Roman seal.   Then
the Sanhedrin could go to prayers and thank God
that "that deceiver" was out of the way.   No more
would he violate their rules and teach heresy to the
people.   No more could he ridicule them to the populace.   Rabbinism and sacerdotalism were still triumphant.   They had saved the Kingdom of God
from this upstart!   They could stroke themselves
with pious satisfaction this Sabbath day.   Did he
brand them "hypocrites"?   He will never do it
again, thank heaven.   Yet, they could still hear
those words ring out in the corridors of the temple
as the people cheered Jesus.   Was he really dead, or
was it all a fancy that he was saying those words
again?   Perhaps their nerves were just a bit over-
strained.   That was all.

8. *Jesus in the Tomb.*—The Sabbath seemed an
eternity.   The excitement had died down.   The
Sanhedrin were grim masters of the situation.
Pilate's flickering conscience worried him at times,
and perhaps his wife still had dreams.   The Roman
soldiers gossiped about the strange prisoner who had
been crucified.   The people of the city had a new respect for the power of the Sanhedrin who after all
had carried out their threat against the Prophet of
Nazareth.   The Galilean multitudes which had

joined so enthusiastically in the triumphal entry accepted the matter philosophically. Many of them said, "I told you so." They always knew that some bad end was in store for this reckless teacher who did not hesitate to oppose the ecclesiastics of Jerusalem. They were the scholars and the custodians of orthodoxy. All that other people had to do was to believe what was doled out to them by the rabbis. Others were sorry and disappointed, but silent. What could they say now?

Jesus was dead. It beat into the soul of Mary, his mother, like the pouring rain. What had the angel Gabriel said? And now this! It was too much for her mother's heart to understand. He was a prophet; he did work miracles; he did claim to be the Messiah, the Son of God. She would believe him against all the world. Besides John the Baptist said that he was the Messiah. Still he is dead. The other women had too much grief of their own to comfort her. And what could they say?

The disciples were scattered like sheep without a shepherd. Judas the traitor had committed suicide. Peter the denier was in tears in secret. John was covering up his own woe in fulfilling Jesus' dying bequest to his mother. The other disciples were not seen after the arrest in the garden. Ah, but they knew what had happened, how they had deserted him in this hour of need.   John alone had been perfectly true and brave in it all, John and the women. The hopes of the disciples lay buried in Joseph's tomb.   No more petty disputes over the chief places in the Kingdom.   To their minds the Kingdom was dead as well as the King.   It was all over with Christianity, for the kingdom of the world had triumphed.   The hope of the world was buried in that tomb.

The enemies of Jesus have manifestly triumphed. It is Satan's triumph and he knew it.   The Sanhedrin had been but tools in his hands, though they piously imagined that they were serving God by what they had done.

There was joy in hell and Jerusalem this Sabbath.   Christ had chosen battle rather than compromise and this is Satan's answer.   Will Jesus remain in that tomb?   Did he remain in that tomb? The light of the world has gone out.   Will that Sun of Righteousness rise again with healing in his wings? On the answer hinges the future of Christianity and the future of the world.   During that Sabbath no one expected it.   All had lost hope and forgotten all that Christ had said on the subject.   The theology of the disciples went down with a crash before the great fact of his death.   That was the outstanding fact that obscured their minds, and that they could not throw off. The funeral knell of the solemn Sabbath hours tolled on the bleeding hearts and hopeless minds of those whom Jesus had chosen for this very day. But they could not raise him from the grave, and to them a dead Christ was a dead Christianity. It is easy for others to offer doctrinaire sympathy in the hour of death as the clods echo our gloom upon the grave. But in this grave lay buried the best flower of the race, the hope of those who had trusted all to him. Put yourself by that tomb and imagine what you could have said. It is vain to recall the promises of a dead Christ.

CHAPTER VIII

THE FINAL TRIUMPH OF JESUS

"The Lord is risen indeed" (Luke 24 : 34).

It was blackness of despair for the disciples. The night was long and there were no stars. True, Jesus had said that he would rise on the third day, but no one thought of that now but his enemies, nor did they believe it. The cruel, blighting, staggering fact of the death of the Master stared them in the face at every turn. He had indeed raised Lazarus from the dead after being in the tomb for four days, but now the grave held Jesus himself fast. With him they had buried all their hopes. It was not a momentary eclipse of faith that had come upon them, but settled night. It is important to realize to the full this situation so that one can see clearly that any light on the matter had to come from someone else than the disciples themselves. No conspiracy on the part of these dejected disciples to revive Christianity with the announcement that Jesus was alive, though he was not, is conceivable. If Christianity was born again with the belief in the Risen Saviour, one must understand how difficult it was

169

for the disciples to come to this belief. If it be said
that the women imagined that they had seen angels
and Jesus, and so restored the hopes of the disciples,
it is to be observed that the disciples did not believe
the women. If it be said that the narratives are
conflicting, one must remember that this shows independence in the testimony. If one says that this is
the after-reflection and theological interpretation of
the disciples, one must recall the fact that the narratives tell unhesitatingly their own blunders, short-
sightedness, lack of faith, difficulty of belief in the
resurrection of Jesus. In simple truth, no theory
has yet been advanced that harmonizes with the fact
of the revival of a dead Christianity save the fact of
the resurrection of Christ. The disciples saw Jesus.
To say that they saw his spirit, not his body, does
not make it easier of belief. It is a miracle to see a
disembodied spirit. Let us linger over the frag-
mentary narratives of the events of those wonderful
forty days. The hopes of the human race centre in
what took place at this time. Let us observe the
steps toward the light.

1. *The Fact of the Empty Tomb.*—This was the
discovery of the women and admitted by all. It is
the first cardinal fact in the new situation. The
enemies of Christ had overreached themselves in
having the Roman seal on the tomb and the Roman

guard to watch it. That guard guaranteed that no man could steal the body of Jesus. When the affrighted soldiers fled to the Sanhedrin, not to Pilate, they told the truth. They said that Jesus came out of the tomb. Did the Sanhedrin believe in Jesus? Not much. Christ had said that they would not believe though one rose from the dead. The Sanhedrin had killed Jesus, and now undertook to kill the fact of his resurrection. A fact is the hardest thing in the world to destroy and has perpetual power of rejuvenation. It is far easier to kill a man than a fact. But Jesus did not appear to the Sanhedrin and they ceased to worry, for the soldiers were compelled for their own safety to say what they were told to say. One may remark in passing that, if the soldiers were really asleep, they knew nothing about what had happened. The Sanhedrin took care of them with Pilate. But to return to the women. Late on the Sabbath afternoon the group of faithful women gave themselves the sad privilege of viewing the sepulchre again. For some reason they did not observe the Roman guard, perhaps not going close enough. After sundown they bought spices with which to anoint the body of Jesus, and then rested till morning. With the dawn they started, doubtless, from Bethany, and before they reached the knoll north of Jerusalem, the sun was risen. They

had made no plan for rolling away the stone, and all
of a sudden they are troubled over that. But, lo,
the stone is already rolled away! What could it
mean? Had his body been stolen by his enemies?
Their ignorance of the guard would make such a suggestion natural to them. They entered timidly
the open tomb and behold two men. At a glance
they see that Jesus is not there. This is the first
indisputable fact that stands out and confronts us.
The empty tomb calls for explanation.

2. *The Story of the Angels.*—The two men turn
out to be two angels and they have an interpretation
of the situation. They offer an explanation of the
empty tomb. The strength of this evidence is
weakened for some minds by the fact that angels are
brought into the narratives. But if men can rise
from the dead, it may be possible for angels to appear
also. Still, it is indirect, for the women have only
heard the angels say that Jesus is risen. "Why
seek ye the living among the dead? He is not here
but is risen" (Luke 24 : 5 f). It is the angels who
seek to remind the women of the forgotten promise
of Jesus that he would rise on the third day. They
now begin to understand. Strange they had not
thought of it before. The women are charged with
a message to the apostles and Peter in particular.
Jesus promises to meet them in Galilee as he had

said he would before his death (Mark 14 : 28).
The women were naturally agitated. Astonishment,
fear, trembling, joy, haste seized them and they ran
in silence on their mission. Was it all true? The
women at least seem to be convinced that Jesus was
alive. But what will the disciples think of it?

3. *John's Intuition.*—The sceptics of the resurrection of Jesus were his own disciples. The problem of the Risen Christ was how to convince them of
this fact. It was impossible to revive faith and hope
in them while they looked on Jesus as still dead.
The resurrection of Christianity depended on the
Risen Christ as a fact and as a force. Mary Magdalen quickly caught the fact that the tomb was
empty and hurried on, without seeing the angels,
to tell Peter and John. Peter is with John now, no
longer alone. Common grief has brought Peter
back. They are both greatly distressed over the
idea that the body of Jesus has been stolen from the
grave, as Mary supposed. They must first see if it
be true. John reached the tomb first, both far out-
running Mary, but hesitated about going in after
seeing the linen clothes lying to one side. Peter
did not hesitate to go in, whereat John did likewise.
John noticed that the napkin that had been on his
head was not with the linen clothes, "but rolled up
in a place by itself" (John 20 : 7). To this sensitive

spiritual temperament here was evidence that Jesus
had indeed risen from the grave. It was no grave
robbery, no sign of a struggle with the guard or
haste in the removal of the clothes, which indeed
would probably not have been removed at all in such
a case. Jesus himself laid that napkin carefully to
one side. "He saw and believed." But Peter was
more matter of fact and still doubted. Peter and
John had both forgotten the pledge of Jesus that he
would rise on the third day, had forgotten indeed the
glory of the transfiguration mount. But if he was
risen, where was he? No one had seen Jesus. It
was still an unsolved mystery. The soldiers alone
knew what had taken place and they did not tell the
disciples but the Sanhedrin. The mouths of the
only eye witnesses to the salient facts were closed.
Possibly the Sadducees had not believed what the
soldiers had said, but the Pharisees had taken it more
seriously. It was a grave situation on the whole.
Were they to be baffled after all? Perhaps, however, he had appeared only as a spirit and had van-
ished to bother them no more.

4. *Jesus and Mary.*—After Peter and John had
left the empty tomb, Mary arrived, for they had been
too swift for her. Another interesting item is the
fact that the angels did not appear to Peter and John,
but reappeared to Mary. One might argue that

this proves that the women started it all out of their excited imaginations, but no one believed the women till their testimony was confirmed. So another solution must be sought, though I have none to offer. Gabriel appeared to Joseph as well as to the mother of Jesus. Mary was standing without, weeping in inconsolable grief. It was bad enough before, but now it is far worse. To have dishonored his body was to go to the last extremity of shame. She stooped and looked into the tomb. The angels are surprised at her grief and she at their joy. She gave the angels the same answer of perplexity concerning what had been done with the body of Jesus, and then turned and saw one whom she took to be the gardener. Here, perhaps, was a ray of light. Possibly he had removed the body of Jesus to another part of the garden. The very soul of Mary went out in her reply when she said: "Sir, if thou hast borne him hence, tell me where thou hast laid him, and I will take him away" (John 20 : 15). It was a pathetic appeal. The answer was the first word that Jesus is known to have spoken to a human being since his resurrection and it was simply "Mary." But it was the old accent and tone of voice. She had not been thinking it possible that Jesus was alive and did not recognize him. Besides Christ had another appearance to some extent. It was not easy to apprehend him at first, and sometimes he held the disciples back in a sense from knowing him. But now there was no doubt. By the open grave Mary saw Jesus. She could only say, "Rabboni." She ventured to lay her hand tenderly upon him, but he restrained her. He is here at all because he has not yet ascended to the Father.

He is on the way from the grave to glory and stops some days with the disciples. He calls them "My brethren" and identifies himself in sympathy with them in relation to God the Father. He sends a message to them that he is going to ascend to the Father. The other women had a promise from the angels that he would see them in Galilee. Both messages were true and would test them. Mary is all ablaze with the wondrous reality and comes running to the disciples with the tremendous words, "I have seen the Lord" (John 20 : 18). But no one believed her. If John heard this, he kept quiet. Doubt held the apostles fast. It simply could not be true. It was some new delusion that had seized Mary. Perhaps the demons had her again.

5. *Jesus and the Other Women.*—He met the women on the way from the tomb with the message of the angels before they had seen the disciples though Luke 24 : 9 may indicate that they had delivered the message of the angels. Jesus repeats the

message of the angels to them that he would meet them in Galilee. And yet he was soon to see them in Jerusalem. Was it that he was gradually getting them ready for seeing him? Before the great reunion in Galilee they would need much strengthening. His appearances to them in Jerusalem were all in the nature of a surprise. The Synoptics all give the Galilee appointment and some of the Jerusalem appearances on this first day also. No more did the apostles believe the testimony of the group of women. It was to them as idle talk (Luke 24 : 11).

6. *Unexpected Light on the Problem.*—Cleopas and a friend lived at Emmaus, some eight miles west of Jerusalem. They had come into town this first day of the week to see if there were any developments among the disciples on the situation. It was late afternoon and they were plodding their way home with heavy hearts. It was still all dark in Jerusalem. They were talking it all over as they went along. It was a time for reviewing the whole career of Jesus of Nazareth. Each sought to explain the work of this marvellous man and asked the other questions on difficult points. Why was there so much promise if it was all to end thus?

A stranger joined them and listened to their talk. Finally he asked what it was all about. "They stood still, looking sad" (Luke 24 : 17). Where

had he been these days not to have heard of Jesus
of Nazareth? Had he lived all alone in Jerusalem?
There was but one theme on people's lips in these
days and that was Jesus. They briefly recounted the
story of the Nazarene, his works, his character, and
his end. They added what had been their own
hope about him, a hope now buried in the tomb.
"We were hoping that it was he that should redeem
Israel." The nation's hope had risen fast around
him. It did look once as though he were the long-
looked-for Messiah. But now it is all over, for he
has been dead three days. It is true that some of
the women had a story that the tomb was empty,
which turned out to be so, but nobody believed what
they said about a vision of angels who alleged that
Jesus was alive. When they left town, no one had
seen Jesus himself.

The stranger now began to talk. He took up the
Old Testament and explained how the career of
Jesus, as they had outlined it, tallied with the description of the Messiah in the Scriptures. He even
argued that it was necessary for the Messiah to
suffer. It was a new and very interesting interpretation to them and they would consider it. It was
wonderful, for their hearts burned as he spoke.
They had never heard it put that way before. But
they are at home and must stop. The stranger hesi-

tated and started to go on.   Only upon their urgent
invitation did he stop for the evening meal.   Across
the table they now sat and he took the bread and said
grace.   It was the old voice and the old charm.
They looked at each other and he was gone!   It
was Jesus, and they had seen him.   The women
were right after all.   Christ had risen from the dead
and was alive.   They must tell the brethren in Jerusalem and bring joy to their hearts.

7. *A Conference on the Situation.*—It was in the
same upper room where they had assembled on that
fateful night when Jesus had foretold all that had
come to pass.   Probably Simon Peter was the cause
of the meeting.   The women had brought a special
message from the angels for him from the Master.
But to crown it all Jesus himself had appeared to
Simon Peter.   The news created the utmost excitement among the apostles.   He was the leader and
surely he would not be deceived, even if the women
had been.   It was a crisis of Christianity, the crisis
of all crises.   If Jesus was indeed risen from the
dead, then all was not lost: in truth, all was won.
There would still be a future, a glorious future,
for Christianity.   It was important that the apostles
do not disband.   They must meet at once with those
disciples that could be reached and confer on the
next step.   Probably Mary and other women were

here also, but Thomas was absent. Possibly in
the hurry he could not be found. There would certainly be an interesting time with all these personal
witnesses to the fact that Jesus was alive. Perhaps
Mary, the other women, Peter, all told how he looked
and what he said. What had Jesus said to Peter?
It was the first time that Peter had seen the Master
since the denials. The rest would eagerly weigh
all that was said. Was it valid evidence? Was it
conclusive? Could they not be mistaken after all?
In the midst of the meeting the two disciples from
Emmaus come with their wonderful story. Before
they can tell it, they are greeted with the glad announcement: "The Lord is risen indeed, and hath
appeared to Simon" (Luke 24 : 32). This last was
the salient point to the disciples. Then the two went
on with their remarkable confirmation. It did indeed look as if it were true, wonderful though it was.
The doors had been shut for fear of the Jews, for
they must take no chances.

As they talked of Jesus all at once he stood in
the midst of them. He had risen from the dead!
But were they now convinced? A strange reaction
set in, for they were now terrified and supposed that
they saw a spirit or ghost, just what some modern
critics now allege. This entire appearance as recorded by Luke and John opposes the idea that it

was only the spirit of Jesus that was seen by the disciples. He showed them his hands and his side and expressly alleged that he was not mere spirit, but even had "flesh and bones" (Luke 24 : 39).

This passage adds to the difficulty, one must admit, for flesh and blood will not enter heaven. The resurrection body is a spiritual body. But one must remember that the case of Jesus is entirely exceptional. He spent forty days on earth between the resurrection and the ascension. His body was not as it had been nor as it would be. He could go through closed doors and yet eat broiled fish. We must leave that mystery unsolved, as we have to do with all the deeper mysteries of God and nature. But after all this is no more difficult than the fact of resurrection, and we can see how this transition state could be a mighty help to the faith of the disciples. Their doubt was so great on this occasion that Jesus upbraided their unbelief. As one has quaintly said, they doubted that we may believe. At last our Lord had convinced his own disciples that he was no longer dead, but alive. It is well for us that the proof was conclusive, for the resurrection of Jesus is the foundation of all our hopes and struggles. Christ has convinced them, but this is only the beginning. They have a mission to the world to go and win it. As the Father had sent him, so he now

sends them (John 20 : 21). They are to announce
to men the terms of forgiveness. Their task is now
to convince others. Can they prove to others that
Jesus is alive, that Christianity is alive also and
destined to conquer the world? They have at least
one qualification; they believe it themselves. They
have hope and faith, but they lack experience and
power.

8. *The Case of Thomas.* — They soon meet
Thomas, who was absent on the Sunday night when
Jesus appeared to the company in the upper room.
They try to convince him by saying: "We have
seen the Lord" (John 20 : 25), and fail utterly to
move his unbelief. He was still as sceptical as they
had been before Peter's experience and before they
had seen the prints of the nails in Christ's hands
and feet. I will not believe, Thomas bluntly said, till
I see what you claim to have seen. After all Thomas
was not much more sceptical than the rest had been
even after they had Jesus right before their eyes.
It is true that he had their testimony added to all
the rest. There is an honest doubt which is the foe
of all credulity. Christianity is the foe of idle super-
stition as well as of blatant infidelity. Christianity
wishes its adherents to look the facts in the face.
Still the disciples had all carried their doubt too far
and were openly rebuked by Jesus for it. Thomas

is not a comfort to the man who prides himself on his scepticism. Jesus was good to Thomas. On the next Sunday the disciples meet again in the same upper room where Jesus had appeared to them just a week before. They have not seen him during the week, for Christ does not remain with them bodily now though he is with them in spirit. Will he come to-night? Who can tell? They have not yet gone to Galilee because the time had not arrived for that. They have not wavered in their conviction that Jesus is alive. They have not formulated any plans for the future of Christianity, but are waiting for further developments. The doors are closed again, for the rulers must be kept in ignorance of the present situation. Thomas is there to-night.

Suddenly Jesus stood before them again and speaks to Thomas. He had accepted the challenge of doubt and showed his hands and his side. It was enough and Thomas could only say to him, "My Lord and My God" (John 20 : 28). If Thomas had doubted longer, his faith now grew faster than that of the rest. He hails Jesus as Lord and God without any reservation. Christ allowed himself to be declared divine, and added that the greatest faith was that which would reach this height without having seen him, the faith of those who "have not seen and yet have believed." This

beatitude belongs to all of us who are convinced of
the resurrection and deity of Jesus.   John adds here,
as if closing his Gospel, that this is the reason why
he has written, to bring to pass just this state of faith
in Jesus as the Messiah, the Son of God.   Surely
his ambition has been nobly realized even though
his Gospel for that very reason has been fiercely
assailed through the ages.   But, sooth to say, John
has given us such a picture of Christ as would make
him, if it is not genuine, the greatest creative artist
of all the ages, a thing that no one believes.

9. *By the Sea of Galilee.*—The days went by and
the disciples turned to Galilee.   The time had not
yet come when Jesus would reveal himself to the
body of believers (over five hundred, Paul said) on
the appointed mountain in Galilee.   There was
nothing to do but to wait in the midst of the scenes
of so much of the work of Christ.   At every turn
along the beloved lake they would be reminded of
Jesus.   They had left their all and cast their fortunes
with the new teacher on these shores.   Had it been
worth while?   What has the future in store for them
now?   Truly it had been wonderful.   Most of them
had been fishermen and so one night Peter took the
initiative and said that he was going fishing.   That
was enough to call back the old days.   Six of them
at once offered to go with him.   They fished all

night and had fisherman's luck and caught nothing.
They were used to that and were pulling for the
shore in the early dawn when they saw a figure in the
dim light walking on the shore. A voice came to
them that was strangely familiar, though the word
"children" as applied to them in address was apparently unusual, but John's fine spiritual sense perceived
the truth, he said: "It is the Lord" (John 21 : 7).
The impulsiveness of Peter responded to John's insight and he was soon on the shore beside Jesus.

The scene between Jesus and Peter on the shore
in the early morning is wonderful indeed. It was
after the breakfast of fish and bread that Christ
turned to Simon. One other morning he had sat by
a fire and this of itself was significant to Simon, but
Jesus was pointed enough to bring the whole scene
of the denial back to his all too vivid memory. He
seized the right moment to probe Simon's heart by
three searching questions. It was Simon who had
spoken for the disciples at Cæsarea Philippi. It
was Simon who had said on the night of the betrayal
that, though all men forsook Jesus, yet he would be
faithful even unto death. Time makes short work
of the boaster and now Simon was in poor shape to
say a word. Jesus was gentle, but persistent with
Peter, challenging his superior love and even his
very love itself with the word chosen by Simon. A

question came for each denial and each cut to the heart. The result was gratifying indeed and revealed a humility in Simon not manifest before, but which reappears in I Peter 5 : 1-11. He is now converted after the sifting by Satan and the prayers of Jesus for him have availed. Jesus exhorts him to feed the sheep and he will later urge the elders to "tend the flock of God" (I Peter 5 : 2). Once Peter had promised Jesus that he would die a martyr's death, if need be, and then turned and ran in disgrace. But now that he is humble he will have a martyr's death by and by. But Simon is Simon still in his personal characteristics, and his curiosity leads him to ask about John, "And what shall this man do?" (John 21 : 22). Peter's question bordered upon impertinence and was sharply rebuked by Jesus, though he did not mean that John actually would live till the second coming, a mistake that John takes pains to correct. James and John had once rashly said that they were able to be baptized with Christ's baptism of blood, and James in fact was soon to drink that cup.

10. *On a Mountain in Galilee.*—The location of this mountain we do not know nor the precise date. Doubtless the bulk of the believers are here assembled. There had been time enough for word to reach them. It was a signal occasion, for here were

assembled the people who represented the visible fruitage of the ministry of Jesus, something over five hundred disciples. The grain of mustard-seed had begun to grow and would ultimately cover the earth. This Jesus knew. Some few still doubted, having a hard battle, but most had come already to a militant faith in the Risen Redeemer. Jesus met this goodly company as the Leader of a world-conquering host. No statesman ever outlined such a magnificent programme as Jesus here laid down, the Christian's Charter for the conquest of the world. No general was ever more certain of victory. The sublime optimism of Christ is transcendent when one recalls that his disciples had no money, no weapons, no influence. They had, however, the supreme message and the presence and power of Christ by the Holy Spirit. It is objected by some critics that the great Commission is too ecclesiastical to be genuine, but baptism is the only item that is open to such a charge and no detailed directions are here given for the execution of that command. All that we get elsewhere. It is a missionary propaganda that Jesus here lays upon the hearts of the five hundred men and women, primarily upon them as members of the Kingdom of God, redeemed individuals. The local church is God's appointed means for carrying on the work of the kingdom, but the responsibility rests ultimately on every believer apart from a church's failure, or performance of duty. The disciples are the salt of the earth, the hope of the world, and the future of Christianity rested on their shoulders.

11. *In Jerusalem Again.*—The Apostles now returned to Jerusalem, the scene of their sore discomfiture, yes, but the scene of Christ's triumphant resurrection also. Henceforth Jerusalem, not Galilee, will be the place of their activity. They will seek to win a foothold right in Jerusalem itself, for now they know that God is with them to the end. James, the brother of Jesus, had received a special manifestation and is now a devout believer along with John and the rest. Mary, his mother, has a new song in her heart. She can sing a new *Magnificat,* with a clearer faith. She had indeed seen the salvation of the Lord. Already, then, a nucleus exists in Jerusalem. Lazarus does not appear more in the history, because, perhaps, of the relentless hatred of the rulers toward him for coming out of the tomb.

Jesus meets the disciples again in Jerusalem and takes pains to give them a last lesson in the interpretation of the Old Testament, for he knew the Old Testament. He was, and is, the great interpreter of Scripture for all time. He found himself in the writings of Moses, the prophets, and the Psalms, though he had to open the minds of the disciples before they could see it (Luke 24 : 45). The open mind is as necessary as the open Scripture and more difficult to get. The closed mind is the chief foe of Scripture truth. Jesus expects us to use our minds in the study of the Bible. Once more Christ urged them on to the conquest of the world. That is the main thing. Missions are the very life of Christianity. They must indeed wait in Jerusalem for power from on high with which to win the world. The spiritual dynamo is absolutely necessary. They will soon receive the Holy Spirit and then they must undertake this world enterprise. They are not, however, to tarry in Jerusalem till all of Jerusalem is won. That is not true yet! They are not indeed ready for this world-mission, for they still look for a temporal kingdom (Acts 1 : 6), an error that the Holy Spirit will remove when he comes. Indeed, the disciples will understand Jesus better after he is gone.

12. *A Last View on Mt. Olivet.*—Jesus led the disciples out of the eastern gate, past Gethsemane with its tragic memories, up the familiar slope towards Bethany, beloved Bethany. The view was sublime in every direction, the Jordan, the Dead Sea, Mt. Nebo, Jerusalem, the Mediterranean. "They were looking up" (Acts 1 : 9) and Jesus was giving them a parting blessing. A cloud swept by

and he was gone.   Long after the cloud disappeared the entranced disciples kept gazing into the heaven whither Jesus had gone.

13. *Till He Come.*—Their upward look was interrupted by the word of the two angels that "this Jesus" will so come back in like manner (Acts 1 : 11). He had said so himself.   They now know that he has risen and believe that he will come back.   In a short time they will be under the tutelage of the Holy Spirit and will come to understand the spiritual nature of the Kingdom of God.   And now they worshipped Jesus (Luke 24 : 52) with joy and praise. The task of the disciples is to understand, to interpret, and to obey Jesus.   The Christian world is still engaged in doing these things.   His life and teachings, his death and resurrection, his power over men to uplift and to make god-like, the greatest of all themes, still fill the horizon of the modern world. Science has done wonders, but science is barren beside the life of Jesus.   He has stood the searchlight of minute historical investigation.   Most of all he endures the test of life.   His pitying eye still looks upon us, his powerful hand still reaches out to save. When he came before they crucified him; when he comes again he will be crowned King of Kings and Lord of Lords.   Meanwhile let him rule in all our hearts.   "Amen: come, Lord Jesus."

INDEX